MONTANA

MONTANA BY ROAD

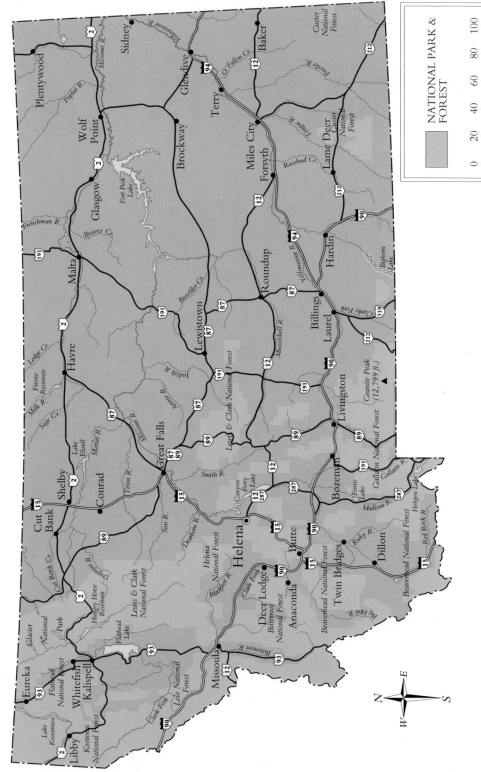

NATIONAL PARK & FOREST

MILES

0 20 40 60 80 100

CELEBRATE THE STATES
MONTANA

Clayton Bennett

BENCHMARK BOOKS

MARSHALL CAVENDISH
NEW YORK

Benchmark Books
Marshall Cavendish Corporation
99 White Plains Road
Tarrytown, New York 10591-9001

Library of Congress Cataloging-in-Publication Data
Bennett, Clayton.
Montana / by Clayton Bennett.
p.   cm. — (Celebrate the states)
Includes bibliographical references (p.) and index.
Summary: An introduction to the geography, history, government,
economy, people, achievements, and landmarks of Montana.
ISBN 0-7614-1312-X
1. Montana—Juvenile literature. [1. Montana.] I. Title. II. Series.
F731.3 .B46   2001   978.6—dc21   2001035970

Maps and graphics supplied by Oxford Cartographers, Oxford, England

Photo research by Ellen Barrett Dudley and Matthew J. Dudley

Cover photo: Chuck Haney

The photographs in this book are used by permission and through the courtesy of:
Corbis: W. Perry Conway, 6-7; David Muench, 10-11, 18, 117; Lowell Georgia, 13, 64; Joseph Sohm, Chro-
moSohm, Inc., 16, 60; Darrell Gulin, 19, 107; Tom Brakefield, 20; Joe McDonald, 21, 23; W. Wayne
Lockwood, M.D., 22; Buddy Mays, 26-27, 106; Galen Rowell, 28, 105; Hulton Deutsch Collection, 58; Brian
Vikander, 62, 65, 86-87; Michael S. Yamashita, 66, 78 (top), 126; Raymond Gehman, 67; Reuters NewMedia
Inc., 68; Annie Griffiths Belt, 70-71; Kevin R. Morris, 73, 74, 139; Dave G. Houser, 79 (right); Bettmann, 89,
130, 132, 135, 136 (right); AFP, 92; Rufus F. Folks, 93; Jacques M. Chenet, 95; Steve Kaufman, 102-103; Dave
Bartruff, 115; Tom Bean, 118; Paul A. Souders, 121 (top); Gunter Marx, 121 (bottom); D. Robert Franz, 124;
Jan Butchofsky-Houser, 128; Cinema Photo, 133; 42, 129. *The Burlington Northern and Santa Fe Railway Com-
pany*: 30-31. *Smithsonian American Art Museum, Washington, DC/Art Resource,NY*: 33. *Montana Historical Society
Museum, Helena*: Don Beatty, 36-37. *Montana Historical Society, Helena*: 38, 40, 46, 47, 50, 52, 99, 131, 134,
136 (left). *Travel Montana*: Donnie Sexton, 54-55, 77, 111. *Mike Byrnes*: 78-79. *Chuck Haney*: 83, 84, 113,
back cover. *©2001 Jeff Schultz/AlaskaStock.com*: 90. *Musuem of the Rockies, Montana State University*: Bruce
Selyem, 96. *Kyle Brehm*, 98.

Printed in Italy

1   3   5   6   4   2

CONTENTS

MONTANA IS . . .

Montana is dramatic.

"When you cross the state line heading west from North Dakota, something changes. Suddenly everything looks farther away, even the sky. The state deserves its nickname 'Big Sky Country.'"

—teacher Kent Warren

Everything about it feels big . . .

"The grandest sight I ever beheld."

—explorer William Clark, on seeing
Great Falls for the first time in 1805

. . . and bold.

"To me Montana is a symphony . . . a symphony of color, painted by a thousand different plants and shrubs which set the hills ablaze—each with its own kind of inner fire."

—politician Mike Mansfield

Montana is part Rocky Mountains . . .

"It is a region of marvelous lakes, towering peaks, vast glaciers and deep, narrow fiords. . . . [Everyone] comes away filled with enthusiasm for their wild and singular beauty."

—conservationist George Bird Grinnell

. . . and part open prairie.

"It is an empty, lonely place if you are not a wheat farmer."

—novelist Richard Ford

In recent years, many newcomers have settled in Montana.

"We drove all around the country, but when I got to Montana I knew it was where I wanted to live. I had found home."
—a New Yorker who moved to Whitefish

Not everyone is happy about it.

"It's a . . . mess now, loaded with boats and people. To me, it's a piece of horror." —author Norman Maclean

But Montana casts a spell that's hard to explain.

"I am in love with Montana. For other states I have admiration, respect, recognition, even some affection, but with Montana it is love, and it's difficult to analyze love when you're in it."
—author John Steinbeck

More than a century ago, Montana became known as the Treasure State because its mountains contained so much gold, silver, and copper. A few people still search for gold. But these days, people are just as likely to be digging for dinosaur bones in Montana as precious metals. Still, Montana has many treasures—awe-inspiring landscapes, hardworking people, and a rich history. Come meet Montana.

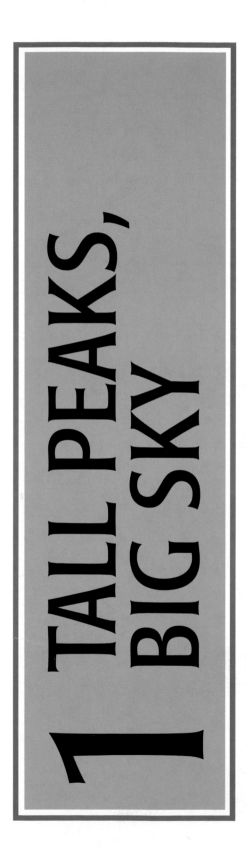

1 TALL PEAKS, BIG SKY

The name *Montana* is based on the Latin word for mountainous, and with good reason. Some of the most impressive ranges of the Rocky Mountains are in the state. But there's much more to Montana. The state also has prairies, badlands, canyons, and grasslands.

It takes a lot of space to hold that many kinds of land, but Montana is more than big enough. It is the fourth-largest of the fifty states. All of New England would fit inside of Montana, with room to spare.

THE ROCKY MOUNTAINS

More than 75 million years ago, huge sections of Earth's crust collided in western North America. As they pushed against each other, land was forced upward, forming the Rocky Mountains. Much later, huge sheets of ice called glaciers covered much of the continent. The glaciers scraped out lakes and valleys as they moved, further changing the landscape.

The Rocky Mountains, which extend from Canada to Mexico, include the western two-fifths of Montana. Many different groups of mountains make up the Rockies. Montana has more than fifty of these mountain ranges, including the Anaconda, Bitterroot, Salish, Gallatin, and Flathead. Many of Montana's jagged peaks soar more than 10,000 feet above sea level. Some are covered with snow for

Western Montana is famed for its high jagged peaks.

LAND AND WATER

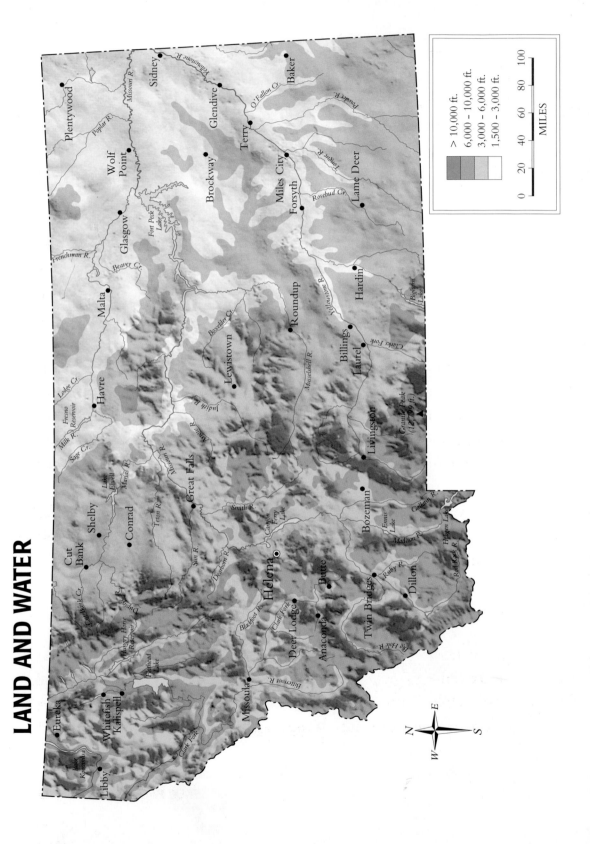

Plentywood

Sidney

Missouri R.

Yellowstone R.

Baker

Glendive

O'Fallon Cr.

Powder R.

Poplar R.

Terry

Wolf Point

Brockway

Miles City

Forsyth

Lame Deer

Tongue R.

Rosebud Cr.

Glasgow

Frenchman R.

Fort Peck Lake

Beaver Cr.

Roundup

Hardin

Bighorn Lake

Malta

Boxelder Cr.

Lewistown

Yellowstone R.

Billings

Laurel

Clarks Fork

Lodge Cr.

Havre

Fresno Reservoir

Judith R.

Musselshell R.

Livingston

Granite Peak
(12,799 ft.)

Milk R.

Sage Cr.

Missouri R.

Missouri R.

Smith R.

Great Falls

Canyon Ferry Lake

Bozeman

Gallatin R.

Lake Elwell

Marias R.

Teton R.

Sun R.

Shelby

Conrad

Ennis Lake

Madison R.

Hebgen Lake

Cut Bank

Dearborn R.

Helena

Butte

Dillon

Ruby R.

Red Rock R.

Cut Bank Cr.

Deer Lodge

Twin Bridges

Dupuyer

Hungry Horse Reservoir

Anaconda

Blackfoot R.

Clark Fork

Big Hole R.

Eureka

Flathead Lake

Whitefish

Kalispell

Missoula

Bitterroot R.

Clark Fork

Lake Koocanusa

Libby

Scale / Legend

> 10,000 ft.

6,000 – 10,000 ft.

3,000 – 6,000 ft.

1,500 – 3,000 ft.

MILES

0 20 40 60 80 100

N
W   E
S

ten months a year. At 12,799 feet, Granite Peak in the Beartooth Mountains is the state's highest point.

Up near Canada, some of the wildest and most scenic parts of Montana have been set aside as Glacier National Park. Several of the ragged peaks in this park are so sharp and remote that they have never been climbed. The park is also famous for the hundreds of deep blue lakes that are nestled between the peaks. "I can't believe this place," says an exhausted hiker from Illinois. "We passed the most incredible waterfalls. Saw a mother bear and two cubs up a tree, then saw a mountain goat. I mean it was right there! And then when we got to Iceberg Lake there were actually icebergs in it! I have to head home tomorrow, but I'm coming back next year."

High up in the Rocky Mountains, many rivers are born as snowmelt tumbles down moss-covered slopes. These trickles eventually turn into cold, fast rivers that are the perfect home for trout. People come from all over the world to fish in the Madison, Gallatin, and Yellowstone Rivers and dozens of other world-class trout streams.

The nation's second-largest river, the Missouri, also starts in the Montana mountains. It roars through a gorge called the Gates of the Mountains before heading out across the plains.

THE GREAT PLAINS

Driving east through the Rocky Mountains you head around jagged peaks and into green valleys, through deep forests and past crystal lakes. Then suddenly the world seems to drop away. Spread out before you are the flat empty Great Plains. "The landscape of

In Montana, the shift from mountains to plains is often very abrupt.

Montana is like what you see on a heart monitor," says Jim Secor, a Lewistown native. "In the west, it has peaks and valleys like a normal heartbeat, and then it goes dead flat." The line where the mountains rise abruptly from the plains is called the Rocky Mountain Front.

The Great Plains cover the eastern three-fifths of Montana. Few trees grow on the rough dry land. "I used to think you had to have trees where you live," says a man from Billings. "But pretty soon you start seeing sunrises, sunsets, and incredible skyscapes." Indeed, without trees or mountains getting in the way, it seems like 90 percent of the world is sky. It is this part of Montana that gives the state its nickname Big Sky Country.

But eastern Montana is not all flat. Scrubby mountain ranges such as the Bears Paw, Big Snowy, and Little Rocky Mountains rise in the middle of the plains. An area called the breaks in the northeast is filled with broken cliffs and ravines. And in the southeast, wind and rain have sculpted the soft earth into amazing pillars and buttes.

WILD THINGS

While the peaks of the Rocky Mountains are indeed rocky, many of the lower slopes are covered with dark green forests of fir, pine, and spruce trees. Cedar, birch, and ash trees are also common. Juniper and cactus survive in some parts of the arid east. Wildflowers such as lupine, heather, and phlox brighten the mountains. Many Montanans say that nothing is more beautiful than a field of bear grass blooming on a mountain slope.

The mountains are home to a huge variety of wildlife, including moose, elk, deer, black bears, grizzly bears, and mountain lions. Glacier National Park is particularly famous for the bighorn sheep and mountain goats that visitors often see darting across its rocky slopes. Montana's grasslands are home to pronghorn antelope, mule deer, and prairie dogs.

Bear grass blooms only once every seven years. One year, just a few of the tall shoots may brighten a mountain slope, while the next year the same slope may be carpeted with blossoms.

Apart from the trout that lure fishers from near and far, grayling, pike, sturgeon, crappie, whitefish, and perch also populate Montana's plentiful waters. Hundreds of types of birds make their home in Montana, from tiny wrens to huge trumpeter swans. All across the state, eagles and hawks soar, keeping an eye out for prey. Many ducks, cranes, egrets, and herons make their homes near lakes, while owls, woodpeckers, and bluebirds flit in the forests.

When bighorn sheep ram horns, it creates a mighty crack that echoes through the mountains.

Mule deer get their name from their huge ears, which look like a mule's.

WINTER AND SUMMER

Because Montana is so far north, many people believe it is always cold. But this is not true. While the average temperature dips near zero frequently in the winter, it does not settle there for the whole season. Instead, mild air often blows in, warming things up. These warm winds, called chinooks, sometimes produce incredibly quick changes in temperature. In Havre, the temperature once rose twenty-six degrees in less than one minute. Another time in Montana, the

Marmots are among the many animals that live in the mountains of western Montana.

temperature shot up forty-seven degrees in just seven minutes.

The eastern plains tend to suffer colder winters than the western mountains. But the mountains get more snow. While people in the east go inside for the winter, for many people in the west, winter is time to play. "It's my favorite season," says a Missoula woman. "I love the peace and quiet—when you get away from all the skiers and snowmobiles. I go snowshoeing and it's like I'm the only person in the world."

A TRUMPETING TRIUMPH

With a wingspan of up to eight feet, the trumpeter swan is the largest waterfowl in North America. These majestic white birds used to live all over Canada and as far south in the United States as Missouri. But hunting and human activities took a harsh toll. By 1932, fewer than a hundred trumpeter swans remained in the world. Most were in Montana's southwestern corner.

Trumpeter swans are very particular about where they nest. These shy birds need a large, quiet area on a lake or stream with no humans around. If someone invades their nesting area, they will let out loud trumpets, bob their heads, and raise their wings. If they are bothered too often, they will abandon their nest entirely.

In 1935, the Red Rock Lakes National Wildlife Refuge was established to give the swans some peace and quiet. Over the years, this remote corner of Montana has given the trumpeters a chance to rebound. Today, more than five hundred nest at Red Rock Lakes and two thousand others arrive each winter from Canada.

In Montana, winter is a great time to play, even for wolves.

The plains also have more severe weather in the summer, where temperatures often soar near a hundred degrees and fierce thunderstorms rumble through. Summers in the mountains are usually cooler and very pleasant. But even on the plains, the heat is more bearable than in some parts of the country because it is not humid and sticky. "The hottest summer day in Montana is never suffocating like a summer day in Washington, D.C.," says Montana writer Norma Tirrell. The state as a whole averages only fifteen inches of precipitation a year, but the west is wetter than the east. In dry years, the plains sometimes get less than ten inches of rain.

PEOPLE ON THE LAND

Because so little rain falls in eastern Montana, the land is often cracked and barren. Livestock can graze here if each animal has

TEN LARGEST CITIES

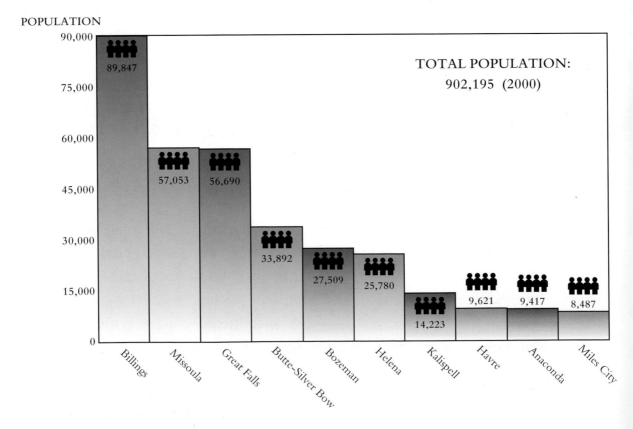

POPULATION

TOTAL POPULATION: 902,195 (2000)

Billings 89,847
Missoula 57,053
Great Falls 56,690
Butte–Silver Bow 33,892
Bozeman 27,509
Helena 25,780
Kalispell 14,223
Havre 9,621
Anaconda 9,417
Miles City 8,487

plenty of space, but farming is difficult at best. As a result, this part of the state has never been heavily populated. Still, Billings, an agricultural center on the Yellowstone River, is the state's largest city. In the west, early mining camps turned into Butte and Helena, while Missoula began as a logging center.

Montana is one of the most sparsely settled states. Three times as many cows live there as people. Only 900,000 people live in all of Montana, which works out to just six per square mile, a smaller number than in any state except Alaska. Despite Montana's small population, people have changed the state's environment dramatically.

Millions of bison, also known as buffalo, once roamed the vast Montana prairie. Most were slaughtered in the nineteenth century as whites entered the region. The few bison that survive in Montana today live on protected reserves or private ranches. As farmers and ranchers took over the plains, other animals were pushed west. The grizzly bear was once a plains animal. But the mountains of western Montana are now one of the few places in the country where you can see these mighty creatures, which weigh up to eight hundred pounds.

People have also changed the face of the land itself. To get at Montana's vast reserves of copper and coal, mining companies used a method called open-pit mining. They simply scraped away the earth's surface, leaving a huge hole in the ground. Mining companies also used so-called heap-leach mining to get at precious metals. They soaked heaps of crushed rock with a poison called cyanide. The cyanide separates the metal from everything else. It also poisons the water and soil. Some mining operations have left

Billings, Montana's largest city, has fewer than 90,000 residents.

Clear-cutting takes down every tree, no matter how small, but it is rarely used today.

open ponds of cyanide that will take years to clean up.

Loggers also changed Montana. First they cut the trees that were easy to reach, on the gentle slopes. After those were gone they moved on to the steeper slopes in the mountains. The least expensive way to harvest timber on steep slopes is by clear-cutting—taking down everything instead of choosing only the best trees. This not only leaves ugly, barren hillsides but also pollutes streams and disturbs animals.

In the 1970s, Montanans became more concerned about the future of their state's environment. Ordinary citizens and politicians began arguing against the use of clear-cutting. They reasoned that they lost more in their quality of life and in money earned from tourism, than the harvested trees were worth. Today, clear-cutting is rare.

Between open-pit mining, heap-leach mining, and clear-cut logging, the face of Montana has been badly scarred. No one knows how long it will take to recover. Today, many Montanans believe that the Treasure State's greatest treasure is its natural beauty. But they will have to work hard to make sure that it is passed on to future generations.

2 PAST AND PRESENT

Looking South from Piegan Pass, by John Fery

Scientists believe that people first came to Montana about 10,000 years ago. They probably survived by gathering wild plants and hunting bison. Over the centuries many other groups came to Montana. Some just passed through; others stayed. Together they make up Montana's rich and colorful past.

NATIVE AMERICAN LIFE

Many different Indian tribes were living in Montana by the time Europeans first arrived there in the 1700s. The Flathead, Kalispel, and Kootenai lived in the Rocky Mountains, where they fished, caught small animals, and gathered roots and berries. On the Great Plains, the Assiniboine, Blackfeet, Northern Cheyenne, Crow, and Gros Ventre were buffalo hunters. Rather than staying in one place, they traveled around, going wherever the hunting was best. They lived in cone-shaped tepees that were easy to take with them. Other tribes, such as the Cree, Nez Perce, Shoshone, and Sioux, traveled in and out of the region, hunting buffalo and other game.

When Indians killed buffalo, they used every part of it. The hide was made into clothing and tepees; the meat was cooked or dried for use later; the bones were carved into tools; and the fat was saved for cooking. Even the buffalo's droppings were used as fuel for cooking fires.

Buffalo Chase, *by George Catlin. The buffalo hunt was central to the Plains Indians' way of life.*

CHANGING HANDS

In the 1600s, France was one of the most powerful countries in the world. French explorers who ventured across North America considered the land theirs for the taking. France claimed much of the continent in 1682. That land, which they called the Louisiana

A CROW LEGEND

Coyote appears in many Native American stories. In this Crow legend, he creates the world.

In the beginning, before there was anything else, Old Man Coyote stood alone, surrounded by water. Two ducks swam near him, and Coyote asked if they had seen anyone else. The ducks said no, but they thought something might be under the water.

Coyote asked them to go under the water and tell him what they saw. They found nothing, so he asked them to go back. The ducks returned with some roots the second time, and with some mud the third time. Coyote told the ducks to build with the mud, and he made an island out of it. He blew on the island to make it grow. It grew and grew until it became the earth. The ducks thought it was too empty, so Coyote made grass and trees out of the roots.

Coyote and the ducks gave the earth lakes, rivers, mountains, and valleys. But still they were not satisfied. So Coyote took more of the mud and created men and women, and more ducks.

One day, Old Man Coyote was traveling and met another, younger coyote. The young coyote wanted Old Man Coyote to make more animals than just ducks and humans. The older coyote agreed. He created other animals without even using mud. He spoke the names of new animals—"Elk! Bear!"—and they appeared as he spoke. This is how all animals were created.

Territory, stretched from the Mississippi River to the Rocky Mountains, and included much of modern-day Montana.

Life in Montana did not change much after France claimed it. Few Europeans even entered Montana in the next hundred years. The Indians continued to hunt bison and fish as they always had. But farther east, dramatic change was happening. In 1776, the American colonies along the Atlantic coast declared their independence from England. They eventually won the Revolutionary War. A new nation was born.

In 1803, the United States purchased the vast Louisiana Territory from France. President Thomas Jefferson quickly organized a team to explore the territory. The group, led by Meriwether Lewis and William Clark, left St. Louis, Missouri, in 1804. They traveled up the Missouri River in hopes of finding a water passage to the Pacific Ocean.

By the time they reached what is now Montana, they realized that the Missouri River would not lead them to the ocean. Instead, they discovered that the mighty river starts in Montana, where three small rivers come together. At this point, they could no longer travel by water. They traded their canoes to some Indians for horses and continued west, across the Rockies and on to the Pacific.

On their return east in 1806, Lewis and Clark passed through Montana again. This time, the team split up. Lewis led one group north, along the Marias River, and Clark led the other group south, along the Yellowstone River. The groups joined together again at the Missouri River and traveled from there back to St. Louis. By the end of their travels, they had explored more of Montana than any other white men.

TRADERS AND TRAPPERS

Lewis and Clark brought back reports of rich lands full of wildlife. Montana, they said, "is richer in beaver and otter than any country on earth." This caught the attention of fur trappers, since they could sell the furs in Europe, where beaver hats were all the rage.

Trading posts were built along rivers. At the posts, Native Americans and trappers known as mountain men exchanged the pelts for the supplies they needed to live in the wilderness. The demand for

Lewis and Clark met the Flathead Indians at Ross Hole, in the Bitterroot Valley. The Indians told the explorers about the best route across the towering mountains. Painting by Charles M. Russell.

beaver pelts was so great that by 1850 trappers had killed nearly all the beavers in North America.

Although the beaver trade dwindled, trading posts continued to operate. They served people who came to the region to hunt buffalo, build cattle ranches, and mine gold and silver. Fort Benton, built on the Missouri River in 1847, became a destination for newcomers who hoped to make their fortunes in the territory.

TREASURE IN THE GROUND

After gold was discovered in California in 1849, thousands of people moved to the West Coast hoping to strike it rich. Others looked for gold and silver in Colorado, Nevada, Montana, and Alaska. Most of them did not find gold, but that did not keep them from trying.

Some Native Americans in Montana knew where to find gold. But since they did not use it for money, they had no reason to dig it

Fort Benton began as a trading post where Indians, particularly Blackfeet, brought their goods to trade. In later years, tons of gold would be shipped down the Missouri River from Fort Benton.

up. A trapper named François Finlay is said to have discovered gold in 1852 at a place called Gold Creek. Apparently, he kept it a secret. He didn't want to ruin the area for fur trapping.

In 1858, James and Granville Stuart found traces of gold, also at Gold Creek. This encouraged others to keep searching. A few years later, in 1862, large gold deposits were found at Grasshopper Creek. News of the discovery spread quickly, and fortune seekers raced to Montana.

Almost overnight, the mining camp at Grasshopper Creek became the city of Bannack. Other mining camps sprouted at each new place that gold was discovered. Some of these towns disappeared when the gold ran out. Others have endured. For example, Last Chance Gulch is now Helena, Montana's capital.

With millions of dollars worth of gold being unearthed in Montana, outlaws soon arrived. They robbed and killed miners and traders. Some towns had sheriffs, but often they were of little help. One of the deadliest gangs, the Innocents, was led by Henry Plummer, a sheriff. The Innocents killed more than one hundred people before a group of citizens took the law in their own hands. They caught Plummer in 1864 and hanged him at Bannack.

Montana's wildness caught the attention of lawmakers back east. To bring the area under control, the U.S. Congress declared Montana a territory in 1864. Federal law enforcement officers came to the territory, and courts were established to try criminals. As order was brought to the area, more merchants and craftspeople decided to take a chance on moving west, hoping to sell their wares in the mining camps. The camps were becoming cities; the territory would soon become a state.

Last Chance Gulch, which eventually became Helena, was named by four unlucky miners who thought the spot was their "last chance" to strike it rich. Their luck turned when Last Chance Gulch turned out to have Montana's second-largest gold deposits.

TOWARD STATEHOOD

As mining towns grew, other settlers followed and built houses, ranches, and farms. Soon settlers were arriving by the thousands.

Conflict with the Native Americans who already lived there was inevitable.

The U.S. government had signed treaties with Native American tribes, promising to keep settlers out of certain areas, saving them for Indians. But as more people wanted to move west, the government took land from the Indians and gave it to white settlers, forcing the Indians onto ever smaller pieces of land.

To make sure the Indians left, the government cut off supplies and encouraged people to kill as many buffalo as they could. Without the buffalo, many Indians starved. Some agreed to move to the reservations that the U.S. government set aside for them. Others stayed to defend their homelands.

The U.S. Army was sent out to round up the Indians who refused to move onto the reservations. But the Indians fought back. One of the most famous battles took place in June 1876. Thousands of Sioux, Cheyenne, and Arapaho were camped along the Little Bighorn River in southeastern Montana. On June 25, Lieutenant Colonel George Armstrong Custer led 225 men into battle against the Indians. In less than an hour every single white soldier was dead. To this day, people debate why Custer was so foolish as to attack when he faced such overwhelming numbers. No one will ever know for sure.

While the Indians won the battle, they lost the war. Custer's humiliating defeat caused the U.S. Army to step up its campaign against the Indians. Within a decade, most Indians had been forced onto reservations.

Montana saw many rapid changes in the 1870s and 1880s. The mining industry grew to include silver, copper, and coal. More and

George Armstrong Custer was famously fun-loving. Another army officer, Theodore Lyman, said that Custer "has a very merry blue eye, and a devil-may-care style."

more settlers arrived, building railroads and towns. Ranchers brought herds of beef cattle to graze on the grasslands of eastern Montana. The Wild West was being tamed. On November 8, 1889, Montana became the forty-first state.

MORE THAN GOLD

Most prospectors who came to Montana hoped to find gold, but one found something better. In the 1880s, Marcus Daly saw that the demand for copper was growing quickly. Miles of copper electric lines and telephone lines were being installed in big cities on the East Coast. In 1881, Daly turned a silver mine near Butte into a copper mine. By 1890, he was selling $17 million worth of copper each year. Daly was suddenly one of the richest men in the country. Another man, William A. Clark, was also mining huge amounts of copper in Butte. The competition between them became known as the war of the copper kings.

Daly and Clark vied to become the most powerful man in Montana. Daly wanted to have the state capitol built in Anaconda, where his mines were based. Clark fought to build the capitol in Helena, where Daly was not as powerful. Clark also ran for the U.S. Senate. The two men spent millions of dollars trying to bribe lawmakers.

Clark won the battle over the location of the new capitol. It was built in Helena, which has been the capital city ever since. But Daly remained rich and powerful until his death in 1900. Though that ended the war of the copper kings, their mining companies remained fierce competitors.

While the copper kings grew rich and powerful, most miners did not. Work in the mines was exhausting and dangerous. Groups of miners formed labor unions in the 1870s to negotiate with mine owners for better pay and safer working conditions. As more miners joined them, these unions became powerful. A mine owner who didn't agree to union terms might lose all his employees to a competitor.

Eventually different factions within the Butte Miners' Union began fighting for control. In 1914, violence erupted. The problem

"CUSTER'S LAST CHARGE"

In 1876, George Armstrong Custer led 225 soldiers into battle against a much larger Indian force. Custer and all of his men were killed. Today, many people think of Custer as arrogant and foolish. But at the time, popular songwriters portrayed Custer as a brave hero, and the Indians as savages.

A - cross the Big Horn's crys - tal tide, a - gainst the sav - age Sioux, A lit - tle band of sol - diers charged, three— hun - dred boys— in blue. In front rode blond - haired Cus - ter bold, pet of the wild— fron - tier: A he - ro of a hun - dred fights, his— deeds known far and near.

2) "Charge, comrades, charge! There's death ahead, disgrace lurks in our rear!
Drive rowels deep! Come on, come on," came his yells with ringing cheer.
And on the foes those heroes charged—there rose an awful yell.
It seemed as though those soldiers stormed the lowest gates of hell.

3) Three hundred rifles rattled forth, and torn was human form.
The black smoke rose in rolling waves above the leaden storm.
The death groans of the dying braves, their wounded piercing cries,
The hurling of the arrows fleet did cloud the noonday skies.

4) The snorting steeds with shrieks of fright, the firearms' deafening roar;
The war songs of the dying braves who fell to rise no more.
O'er hill and dale the war song waved 'round craggy mountain side,
Along down death's dark valley ran a cruel crimson tide.

5) Our blond-haired chief was everywhere 'mid showers of hurling lead,
The starry banner waved above the dying and the dead.
With bridle rein in firm-set teeth, revolver in each hand,
he hoped with his few gallant boys to quell the great Sioux band.

6) Again they charged, three thousand guns poured forth their last-sent ball.
Three thousand war whoops rent the air—gallant Custer then did fall.
And all around where Custer fell ran pools and streams of gore,
Heaped bodies of both red and white whose last great fight was o'er.

The copper beneath Butte made Marcus Daly and William A. Clark rich, but Butte itself was a grim and grimy place.

grew so serious that the National Guard was sent in to keep peace. That same year, the unions were disbanded.

THE LAND RUSH

In 1862, President Abraham Lincoln had signed the Homestead Act. It was meant to encourage Americans to settle the West. For a ten-dollar filing fee, settlers could lay claim to between 160 and 640 acres of government land. If they built a house and stayed on the property for at least five years, the land was theirs.

Filing a claim was easy enough, and there was plenty of land available in Montana. The hard part was making a living. Despite Montana's natural beauty, it was not well suited for farming or ranching. Settlers soon discovered that even 640 acres was not enough to graze cattle or raise crops there.

Few settlers came to Montana for the first several years after the

Unlike more fertile parts of the country, Montana experienced its land rush in the twentieth century. Homesteader Rosie Roesler built this house on her claim in 1912.

Homestead Act was passed. Many people thought it was still too dangerous to live that far west. Mining boom towns were lawless, and Indians still traveled most of the state's open land. Homesteaders only took interest after the territory was declared a state.

The greatest land rush in Montana began in 1908. Railroad owner J. J. Hill promoted settlement in Montana, advertising it as a place of rich farmland and great beauty. Hill controlled three railroads—the Great Northern, Northern Pacific, and Burlington lines. These lines crossed Montana on their way from Minnesota to Washington State. If Montana had more settlers, Hill would have more business for his railroads.

Hill did everything he could to attract new settlers. He ran advertisements all over the eastern United States and Europe. He hired agricultural experts to support his claims about farming in Montana. And he lowered train fares for anyone moving there. Soon people were pouring in.

Miners and cowboys who already lived in Montana were not happy to see so many newcomers. As the cowboys saw it, new residents were spoiling the state's untamed land with their crude farms and houses. Artist Charles Marion Russell grew furious as he watched the plains plowed into fields and surrounded with fences. During a speech in 1923, he tore up his prepared notes and said, "In my book, a pioneer is a man who turned all the grass upside down, strung bob wire all over the dust that was left, poisoned the water and cut down the trees, killed the Indians who owned the land and called it progress. . . . If I had my way, the land would be like God had made it and none of you would be here at all."

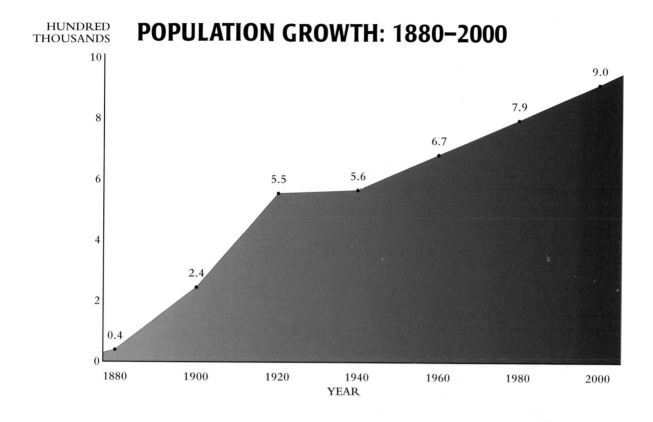

POPULATION GROWTH: 1880–2000

HUNDRED THOUSANDS

0.4 — 1880
2.4 — 1900
5.5 — 1920
5.6 — 1940
6.7 — 1960
7.9 — 1980
9.0 — 2000

YEAR

But the settlers believed that farming and ranching were progress, and for a while they appeared to be right. Weather was good for several years during the land rush, with high rainfall even in the dry eastern part of the state. Wheat harvests were generous, and it seemed Hill's promises had come true. But drought struck Montana in 1917, and farmers struggled. The following year, the rain still hadn't returned. Crops wilted and the rich topsoil turned to dust. Thousands of farms failed that year, and again in 1919. Banks and other businesses that depended on the settlers and their farms soon closed.

Some farmers and ranchers stayed to work the land, and a new

The broad Gallatin Valley was the most productive farming region in Montana.

wave of settlers came to try their luck. They learned to work through the dry periods by planting a variety of crops and using drought-resistant wheat. The number of successful farms grew, and so did the number of land claims. By 1922, settlers had claimed 93 million acres of government land.

Not all government land was up for grabs by settlers. At the request of President Theodore Roosevelt, Congress set aside some areas of natural beauty to become national parks. One of the first was Glacier National Park in northwestern Montana, which was established in 1910.

GOOD TIMES AND BAD

The worldwide economic troubles known as the Great Depression hit Montana hard in the 1930s. The state's coal industry ground to a halt as factories shut down and trains stopped running. At the same time, Montana was suffering through another drought. Prices for farm goods also fell. Another wave of homesteaders gave up. Whole communities moved at once, leaving their land to be reclaimed by someone else.

There wasn't enough business to keep everyone employed. By 1935, one in four Montanans was receiving help from the federal government. Not all government aid was welfare, however. Some miners and loggers were hired to build roads or put up power lines. Others were put to work building the Fort Peck Dam on the Missouri River. When it was completed in 1940, the dam helped provide irrigation for crops and generated power for eastern Montana.

The beginning of World War II revived the state's logging, mining, manufacturing, and ranching businesses. The government needed metal for building materials, coal for fuel, and beef to feed the army. The country was preparing to go to war, and Montana was going back to work.

By the 1950s, most jobs in Montana were in cities rather than on farms or ranches, so most Montanans were city dwellers. But industry also grew in remote areas. Oil was found in the Williston Basin of eastern Montana, and oil wells soon dotted the landscape.

By this time, mining companies were using open-pit mining, where they scraped away the earth to get to the minerals underneath. Montanans were accustomed to huge mining operations near Butte, so they did not object to open-pit mining there. Then in the 1970s, mining companies established huge open-pit mines in southeastern Montana.

During the Great Depression, the U.S. government gave many people jobs building roads, trails, and lodges in the beautiful Montana wilderness.

When people saw the plains torn apart by these mines, they decided it was too high a price to pay for coal. The state legislature passed laws in the 1970s that helped reduce the damage done by open-pit mining. They also raised taxes on the mining companies and used the money to restore the damaged areas.

CAN'T TAKE THAT AWAY

The history of white settlement in Montana has been one of taking things away. First it was beavers, hunted for their pelts. Then it was gold, silver, copper, and buffalo. Then it was prairie land for farming and ranching, and the forests for lumber. Next it was coal and oil. There isn't enough left of some of these things to take any more.

Montana has a much smaller mining industry than it once did. The prairies can't support any more grazing or crops than they already do. Logging in the mountains is expensive. The only things Montana can sell and still keep are its scenery and history.

Tourism is now one of the state's largest industries. People take away memories and photographs, leaving the landscape as they found it for others to enjoy. Tourism is not the most profitable business Montana has had, but it is one that this beautiful but fragile land can support.

3 PUBLIC LIFE

The capitol in Helena

Montana residents are proud of their state's Wild West history. But few would want to go back to the days of outlaw gangs. To keep order and govern the state, Montana needed a set of laws and rules.

The state's first constitution, which lays out the framework for the state government, was approved by voters in 1889. By 1969, it had been revised so many times that Montana voters decided it was time to completely rewrite it. In 1972, a hundred Montanans worked together to create a new state constitution.

INSIDE GOVERNMENT

Montana's government is modeled after the federal government. Each has three branches: executive, legislative, and judicial.

Executive. The governor is the head of the executive branch. He or she signs bills passed by the legislature to make them into laws. The governor also appoints members of state boards and commissions. The state elected its first female governor, Judy Martz, in 2000. Other executive branch offices include lieutenant governor, attorney general, auditor, secretary of state, and superintendent of public instruction. All are elected to four-year terms.

Legislative. The legislative branch is made up of two groups— the house of representatives and the senate. The one hundred representatives in the house are elected to two-year terms, while

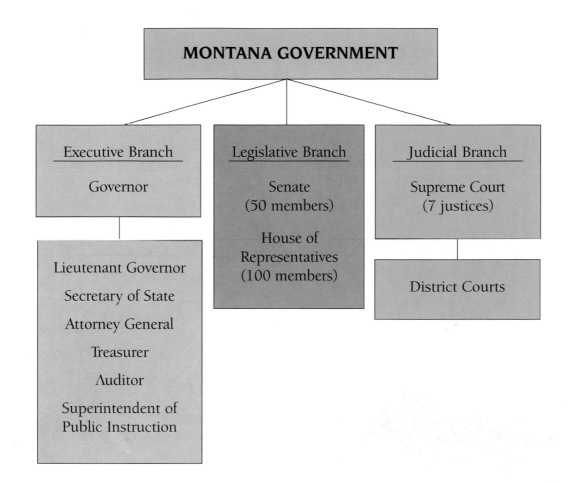

MONTANA GOVERNMENT

Executive Branch

Governor

Lieutenant Governor

Secretary of State

Attorney General

Treasurer

Auditor

Superintendent of Public Instruction

Legislative Branch

Senate (50 members)

House of Representatives (100 members)

Judicial Branch

Supreme Court (7 justices)

District Courts

the fifty senators are elected to four-year terms. The legislators vote on proposed laws, called bills, and approve budgets. After the legislature passes a bill, it goes to the governor for approval. If the governor signs the bill, it becomes law. If he or she rejects the bill, it can still become law if two-thirds of both the house and the senate vote to pass it again.

Judicial. The state's courts make up the judicial branch of government. The state's highest court, the supreme court, has seven justices. All are elected to eight-year terms. The judges who

MONTANA PIONEER

Before most women in the United States were even allowed to vote, a Montana native became the first woman ever to serve in Congress. A former teacher and social worker, Jeannette Rankin had led the effort to get women the right to vote in Montana. In 1916, Montana voters elected her to the U.S. House of Representatives.

In Congress, Rankin fought to get all women in the United States the right to vote. She was also a champion of children's rights and of prohibition, which would outlaw the sale of alcohol. Within a few years, all women in the United States did have the right to vote, and prohibition became law.

Rankin was best known for her opposition to war. She was one of the few members of Congress who voted against the declaration of war on Germany that brought the United States into World War I in 1917. Her decision was not popular with Montanans, and she was not reelected.

But Rankin remained active in politics. She was elected to Congress again in 1940. Again she opposed a declaration of war, this time against Japan for the bombing of Pearl Harbor. Explaining her vote against the United States entering World War II, she said, "As a woman I cannot go to war, and I refuse to send anybody else."

She did not run for reelection. Although she never again held public office, she continued to work for the causes she believed in until her death in 1973.

preside over Montana's nineteen district courts are each elected to six-year terms. Most serious cases are tried in district courts. Less serious cases are handled by municipal courts and justice of the peace courts. If someone believes an error was made in a trial, they can ask the state supreme court to review the case. The supreme court also rules on whether laws violate the state constitution.

CHANGING LAWS

Montana has a reputation as a place where people don't like the government telling them what to do. The state lived up to its reputation in 1995, when the legislature passed a law doing away with daytime speed limits on the state's largest roads. Instead, the law said people were to drive at "reasonable and prudent" speeds.

A lot of drivers decided the law meant they could drive as fast as they wanted. Cars zooming down the road at more than a hundred miles an hour were common. "With no speed limits, it seemed like everything was out of control," says Patti Marnon, a waitress in western Montana. "I've driven into the ditch several times to avoid accidents." Max Johnson of Ravalli agreed. "You can hardly pull out onto the highway," he says. "People can't react at high speeds. It's just nuts."

Many people thought the law just wasn't fair. Who was to say what was "reasonable and prudent?" "What's reasonable to me is not reasonable to you," says one Montanan, "or to Richard Petty," the race car driver. Most police officers decided that "reasonable and prudent" meant between eighty and ninety miles per hour. Eventually, the Montana Supreme Court got involved, ruling that

After Montana did away with a precise speed limit, "People felt like they had permission to drive too fast and had no patience for people driving the regular speed," says Dennis Unsworth of the Montana Department of Transportation.

"reasonable and prudent" was too vague. When a new law went into effect in 1999, giving the state a top limit of seventy-five miles per hour, many Montanans breathed a sigh of relief.

Recently, some Montanans have been seeking to change laws intended to protect the environment. For instance, in 2001 the

Montana legislature considered shortening the time it takes to approve construction of power plants. Many business groups argued that the old laws hurt the economy. They said that companies didn't want to wait a year before building, so they often wouldn't bother to build in Montana at all. People who support the old laws say that speeding up the process won't leave enough time to study the environmental effects of the projects. They fear that it will bring back the days when mining and other companies destroyed the land and polluted the water. "Their whole premise is wrong," says Thomas Power, an economist at the University of Montana. "All they know is they are losing jobs in mining."

Power points out that tourism and outdoor recreation are producing the most jobs in Montana these days. And what attracts

GROSS STATE PRODUCT: $21.47 BILLION (2001 ESTIMATED)

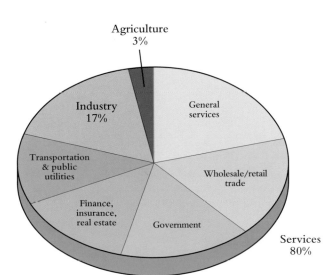

Agriculture 3%

Industry 17%

General services

Transportation & public utilities

Wholesale/retail trade

Finance, insurance, real estate

Government

Services 80%

people to Montana are the pristine mountains and clean trout streams. "These people are staring into the rearview mirror, lost in fantasies tied to the past," argues Power. But making a living in Montana is not easy, so many people are willing to do anything that they believe will bring higher paying jobs to the state.

For every person in Montana, there are 150 trout large enough to be caught.

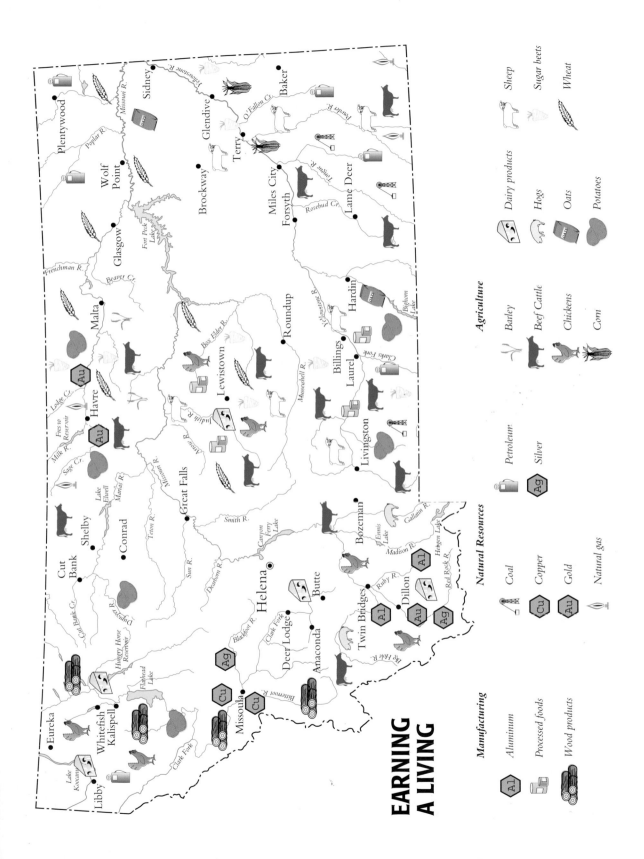

EARNING
A LIVING

Manufacturing

- Al — Aluminum
- Processed foods
- Wood products

Natural Resources

- Coal
- Cu — Copper
- Au — Gold
- Natural gas
- Petroleum
- Ag — Silver

Agriculture

- Barley
- Beef Cattle
- Chickens
- Corn
- Dairy products
- Hogs
- Oats
- Potatoes
- Sheep
- Sugar beets
- Wheat

WORKING IN MONTANA

Although Montana's rough-and-tumble history is filled with miners and ranchers and hunters, today 80 percent of the workers in Montana have service jobs. These include jobs in stores, banks, schools, and hospitals. Jobs in the tourism industry—from working in a motel to running a ski lift to leading raft trips—are also service jobs.

The largest single employer in Montana is the state government. The state employs 24,000 people, ranging from schoolteachers to park rangers to the governor. The U.S. government employs

Many Montanans work for the government, including this park ranger.

There are 2.7 million cattle in Montana. Beef is the state's most valuable farm product.

another 21,000 Montanans. Large private employers include the Montana Power Company, the Burlington Northern Santa Fe Railway, Wal-Mart, and Albertson's grocery stores.

In the early twentieth century, thousands of homesteaders claimed millions of acres in Montana for farming and ranching. Most failed to earn a living from the land. These days, Montana has 27,500 farms that cover more than 57 million acres. Agriculture employs about 8 percent of Montana's workforce.

Farms and ranches cover almost two-thirds of Montana.

Most agricultural land in Montana is used for ranching. Beef and dairy cattle graze the plains. Sheep and hogs are also raised there. Some ranchers now raise buffalo, because they are ideally suited to life on Montana's prairies. Buffalo meat is becoming popular in some places because it has less fat than beef. Wheat is the leading crop in Montana. Other important crops grown in the state are barley, hay, potatoes, and beets.

Making wood products is the state's leading manufacturing industry. Logs become lumber, plywood, telephone poles, and pencils. Oil refining and the production of aluminum, concrete, and machinery are also important businesses in Montana. Food processing, such as meatpacking and turning grain into flour, is big business in Billings and Great Falls.

Despite its importance to the state's history, mining only employs 1 percent of Montana workers today. Instead of hiring thousands of miners to dig metal from the hills, mining companies now use

These logs might be turned into anything from houses to toothpicks.

large machines to get coal, oil, and precious metals from the ground.

EARNING A LIVING

From the mountain men of the early nineteenth century to the men and women who fight forest fires today, Montanans have always been hard workers. Only a few people have grown rich working in Montana, and only then by a stroke of luck in addition to effort. In recent years, Montana workers have earned the lowest wages in the United States. They earn 30 percent less than the national average. With such low wages, 16 percent of the state's residents live in poverty. Many others struggle to make ends meet. "If I could make $10 an hour I'd be happy," says Carrie Villa, a secretary in Helena who is trying to raise two kids on $8.50 an hour. "Then I could set a little bit aside every month."

More jobs have been created in Montana recently, and by 2001, unemployment was at its lowest levels in years. But wages are still low, and many of the jobs offer no benefits or security. It seems that for many people, working in Montana is just the price they pay for the pleasure of living in Montana. "I love this state," says Villa. "It's hard to live here, but you don't live in Montana for the money anyhow."

Few people work as hard as the men and women who fight forest fires. These firefighters are heading out for another day's work after fourteen straight days of fighting a fire in northwestern Montana.

4 THE LAST BEST PLACE

You know you're in the West when you enter Montana. Almost everybody is wearing jeans and cowboy boots, and sometimes it seems like every other car on the road is a beat-up old pickup truck. But there's much more to Montana than what you see at first glance. Look closer and you'll notice the many different ways that people enjoy life in what some call the Last Best Place.

EASTERNERS AND WESTERNERS

The landscapes of eastern and western Montana are very different, and so are the people who live there. They tend to lead different lives and have different outlooks.

Easterners are more likely to work on farms or ranches or in the coal or oil business. Billings, Montana's largest city, is in the east. But generally the eastern part of the state feels more rural, and its people are more conservative. "People here love their God, their families, and their independence," says journalist Becky Bohrer. They are skeptical of the more freewheeling lifestyle of people in western Montana.

Western Montanans are more likely to work in government and education. Tourists flock to Montana's mountains, and so do most people who move to the state from other places. As a result, western

Montana historian Joseph Kinsey Howard once said, "We have room. We can be neighbors without getting in each other's hair. We can be individuals."

Montanans are more used to outsiders. Missoula, in particular, is considered a very open city.

COMMON GROUND

One thing is true of longtime Montanans, no matter what part of the state they call home: they're tough. Living in this beautiful but unforgiving land takes resourcefulness. If the nearest auto repair shop is a hundred miles away, you learn how to fix a car yourself pretty quickly. Montanans also learn to take care of themselves at an early age. Rural kids sometimes learn to drive when they're just fourteen, because they are needed to help out on the farm. And many Montanans teach their children how to handle a rifle long before that.

Montana's size and vast, empty spaces gives some people a feeling of privacy and freedom. As Paul Hundertmark, a grain elevator operator in Billings, says, "If I can't walk out my back door and shoot a gun, I'm in too big a city."

Montanans mostly keep to themselves. They'll help each other, of course, but most of the time they just look after their own families, businesses, and land, and expect everyone else to do the same. They are experienced at being good neighbors while

"You have to value people as the main thing when you live up here," says one northern Montanan.

respecting other people's privacy. An elderly resident of Plentywood boasts, "We still watch out for each other. Nobody steps on anybody else's toes. But we watch out for each other."

In Montana's wide-open spaces, towns are few and far between. What towns there are often have tiny populations with only a few businesses. People in small towns think nothing of driving seventy, eighty, even a hundred miles—one way—to Billings or Great Falls to go shopping or to a movie. Although some people might find life in these towns boring, small-towners often have busy social lives, filled with an endless array of sporting events, fundraisers, and church meetings. They know the people in their town, and that's enough for them. "This life—isolated and quiet—is one they have chosen and one they want to keep," points out Bohrer.

ETHNIC MONTANA

Most Montanans—91 percent—are white. During the mining boom and land rush, large numbers of people from Germany, Ireland, Wales, Norway, and Hungary arrived in Montana. Some Montana towns still have strong ethnic identities, such as Glasgow with its Scottish roots and Libby with its Norwegian Americans.

Butte in particular has strong ethnic ties, which date back to its days as a center of copper mining. The city's Irish heritage becomes apparent each March 17, during its rousing St. Patrick's Day parade. It is one of the nation's largest, although Butte has fewer than 34,000 residents. Many people from Cornwall, the southeastern part of England, also moved to Butte. One of their favorite foods was a meat pie called a pasty, which came in handy because it was easy

ETHNIC MONTANA

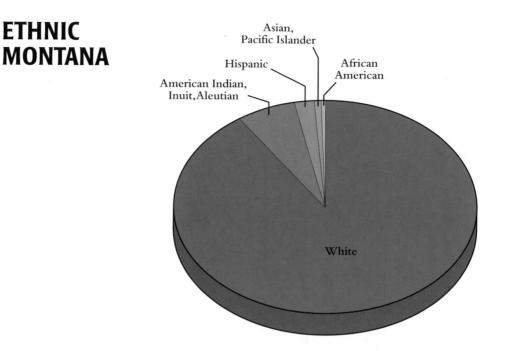

Asian, Pacific Islander

Hispanic

American Indian, Inuit, Aleutian

African American

White

to bring to the mines for lunch. Pasties remain popular in Butte to this day.

Many German immigrants settled on the prairie during the homesteading years. Some were Hutterites, German-speaking people from Russia. They had faced intolerance in Europe because of their beliefs. They share all goods and property and refuse to use guns or serve in the military. Today, about forty Hutterite communities, each with a few dozen residents, are spread across central Montana. To this day, Hutterites speak German, wear old-style clothes, and do not watch television. They continue to live together, raising crops and livestock and taking care of each other.

African Americans, Asian Americans, and Pacific Islanders combined make up only about one percent of Montanans. About 2 percent of Montanans are Hispanic. Billings has the state's largest

Hispanic community. Each August, the city throws a two-day fiesta filled with Mexican music, dancing, games, and food.

Native Americans are Montana's largest minority group, making up more than 6 percent of the population. Members of the Blackfeet, Flathead, Assiniboine, Gros Ventre, Crow, Northern Cheyenne, Chippewa, Cree, and Sioux tribes all live in the state. While most Native Americans in Montana live on the state's seven reservations, every county in the state has some Native American residents.

Montana's Native Americans value their history. They share it through stories and language, songs and dances, arts and crafts, and

St. Patrick's Day is Butte's biggest celebration.

Montana is home to about four thousand Hutterites.

Each year Butte holds a Chinese New Year celebration to honor its Asian heritage.

A boy wears traditional clothing at the Rocky Boy Powwow in north-central Montana.

CHINESE IN MONTANA

At one time, more than 10 percent of Montanans were Chinese. Alone or in families, they came to Montana from California to try their hands at digging for gold. Many of them also helped build the railroads that later carried Montana's products to market. So many Chinese Americans settled in Butte that it is thought the town was one-third Chinese in the early 1900s.

Chinese immigrants made many contributions to the mining industry and the economy of the new state. But they were often treated with hostility. Though several Chinese residents of Butte became successful merchants, the local newspapers made it clear they were not welcome. An editorial in the *Butte Miner* said, "a Chinaman could no more become an American citizen than could a coyote."

When economic times turned tough, many white settlers blamed the Chinese for their troubles. Within a few years, most Chinese in Montana found their way back to the West Coast.

Each year, Butte honors its Asian past with what it proudly proclaims to be the world's shortest and loudest Chinese New Year Parade. Throughout the year, visitors can glimpse the world of the Chinese in Butte at Mai Wah, a museum in the heart of Butte's old Chinatown.

games and ceremonies. Throughout the warmer months, Montana Indians hold gatherings called powwows. A powwow is a combination of cultural holiday, family reunion, and county fair. The largest powwow in Montana is the Crow Fair and Rodeo. People from all around the United States and Canada travel to Crow Agency, sixty miles from Billings, to be part of it. They camp along the banks of

INDIAN FRY BREAD

A traditional dish called fry bread is served at almost every Indian event and restaurant in Montana. Have an adult help you make this tasty snack.

2½ cups flour
1½ tablespoons baking powder
1 teaspoon salt
1 cup warm milk
1 tablespoon vegetable oil
Vegetable oil (for frying)
Cinnamon
Sugar

Stir together the flour, baking powder, and salt in a large bowl. Combine the milk and the tablespoon of oil in another bowl. Stir the liquid mixture into the dry mixture until a smooth dough forms. Knead the dough into a smooth ball, then cover it and let it sit for 10 minutes. Divide it into 8 balls. Flatten each ball until it is 8 to 10 inches across.

Now it's time to cook. Pour enough vegetable oil into a frying pan to cover the bottom and heat over medium-high heat. Place one piece of flattened dough in the frying pan and cook it until it is golden and crisp. This usually takes 1 to 2 minutes for each side. Cook the remaining fry breads. Sprinkle with cinnamon and sugar and enjoy.

the Little Bighorn River, creating the "teepee capital of the world." A parade starts off the activities each morning, and the days are filled with wild horse races, Indian foods, art shows, traditional music and dancing, re-creations of historic events, and a rodeo. "Powwows give people support and strength," says one powwow participant. "Whatever they're coming here for, they usually find it."

THE GOOD LIFE

Most Montanans love the outdoors. It's why they live here. Hunting and fishing are a basic part of the Montana culture. When a Glendive woman included a picture of herself with a dead deer in the back of a pickup with her annual Christmas letter, her relatives on the West Coast found it strange. But to her it was perfectly natural, because in Montana hunting is an everyday and vital part of life.

But there's more to enjoying the Montana outdoors than just looking for dinner. In places like Missoula it seems like every car is carrying a mountain bike or a kayak or skis. "You always want to be ready in case you can get off work a little early," says one woman.

As the fashionable slopes in Colorado and Wyoming get ever more crowded, more and more people from out of state are discovering Montana ski resorts like Big Sky and Big Mountain. Cross-country skiing and snowmobiling are also popular among Montanans. The state has 3,700 miles of groomed snowmobile trails. Most scenic highways are closed to cars in the winter because of snow. But snowmobilers can still get through to visit some of the state's natural wonders in their frozen winter glory.

Hunting is a way of life for many Montanans.

Over the years, more and more people have heard about the good life that Montana offers. In the 1980s, outsiders started buying large chunks of Montana. Ted Turner, a wealthy businessman who owns many cable television channels, established a ranch for restoring

Skiers flock to the Big Mountain Ski Area to take advantage of the three hundred inches of powdery snow that fall there each year.

more bison to the state. Elizabeth Clare Prophet, the leader of a new-age church, built a compound where she and her followers waited for the end of the world. Other property was sold to celebrities such as actor Tom Cruise. Many Montanans were suspicious and resentful of these wealthy newcomers.

Most new Montanans, however, are just ordinary people who want a piece of the Montana lifestyle. Between 1990 and 2000 the state's population grew by 13 percent, to 902,195.

Montanans have grown more comfortable with Ted Turner since he first bought property in the state. His buffalo herds have grown, and he has shown a commitment to the area. Meanwhile, the world did not end when Elizabeth Clare Prophet said it would. Her church lost most of its members, and its land was sold. Just as many of Montana's early settlers did, some newcomers have packed up and gone back home.

But many other new Montanans have stayed. Why leave when they have found paradise? Like the old-timers who wouldn't dream of living anywhere else, they're hooked on Montana's amazing landscapes. As poet Greg Keeler says, "Some of us were born here, and some of us came for the trout."

5 BIG SKY, BIG NAMES

With such a small population, Montana seems an unlikely place to produce so many famous people. But the state seems to bring out the best in its residents. From pioneer artists to Olympic athletes, Montanans have made their mark on the world.

PAINTING THE WEST

More than any other artist, Charles M. Russell captured the spirit of the American West. He created vivid images, full of action. His paintings and sculptures show Montana at its most beautiful, and Montanans at their best.

Russell was born in St. Louis, Missouri, in 1864. From an early age, he heard stories about the West and longed to explore it. He realized his dream at age sixteen, when he headed for Montana. Russell worked on ranches for several years. He wasn't much of a cowboy, but he loved his new home. He was enchanted by the unspoiled landscapes, the cowboys on the open range, and the Indians who still lived in their traditional ways. He hated seeing the prairies fenced off and plowed under.

Russell was constantly drawing, painting, and sculpting images of things he saw in Montana. "Charley loved beauty," his friend Frank Bird Linderman once wrote. "Grace, especially in the forms and movements of animals, fascinated him." Although he became

Charles M. Russell loved how the West was before white settlers arrived. "Those Indians have been living in heaven for a thousand years," he once said, "and we took it away from 'em."

a successful artist, Russell didn't take his artwork seriously. He once said, "I ain't an artist, I'm an illustrator."

MONTANA CHAMPIONS

Each year since 1973, dogsled racers have competed in the Iditarod Trail Sled Dog Race. The race was named after a gold-mining town between Anchorage and Nome in Alaska. Stretching over 1,049 miles, the race is a tribute to sled-dog drivers who carried medicines to miners in Nome during an outbreak of a deadly disease called dyptheria in 1925.

Doug Swingley has dominated the Iditarod Sled Dog Race in recent years. Another racer, Paul Gebhardt, says that for Swingley to lose "He has to have a problem, a big problem, like his sled falling into the ocean."

Until the 1990s, only Alaska natives ever won the Iditarod. But then Doug Swingley, who was born in Great Falls, Montana, entered the field. He had started dogsled racing in 1989, and entered the Iditarod for the first time in 1992. That year he was named rookie of the year. Three years later, in 1995, he won the Iditarod with a record-breaking time of 9 days, 2 hours, and 42 minutes. He broke his own record in 1999, with a time of 9 days, 58 minutes. He won again in 2000 and 2001, becoming one of the most successful dog sled racers of all time. He is the only person ever to win the Iditarod three years in a row.

Swingley lives near Lincoln, Montana, training far from the Alaska landscape where he competes. "I enjoy being out of the loop," says Swingley. "I don't hide out. I am hidden out because they can't see me. It definitely develops a mystique. No one knows what I'm doing here."

Another Montana champion is Olympic skier Eric Bergoust. He does things most skiers won't even try. Growing up in Missoula, Bergoust loved excitement. More than anything else, he wanted to fly through the air. He even convinced his younger brothers to jump off the roof of his family's two-story house onto an old mattress. So when he learned about aerial skiing, which has competitors flipping through the air, he had to try it. He and his brothers built their own ski jumps. "I just loved to jump. I had faith and determination I would figure it out someday," he says.

His dedication eventually led him to the top of his sport. He won a gold medal at the 1998 Olympics. He has also won three U.S. championships.

Bergoust gets better every year because he's not just a daredevil.

"This sport can teach kids to believe in themselves . . . to follow their dreams and enjoy what they do each and every day," says aerial skier Eric Bergoust.

He works hard for every victory. Bergoust says of his success, "The thing I'm most proud of is how hard it was to achieve."

MAKING MOVIES

Director David Lynch is known for bringing dark, strange stories to the screen. His movies often show violent struggles between good and evil in small-town settings. Lynch, however, is not strange at all. He was born in Missoula in 1946, and had a normal childhood. He even became an Eagle Scout. He eventually went to art school to study painting before turning to film.

Lynch is best known for the movies *Eraserhead*, *The Elephant Man*, and *Blue Velvet* and the television series *Twin Peaks*. His movies

David Lynch once said that many of his films take place in "strange worlds that you can't go into unless you build them and film them. I just like going into strange worlds."

always include mysterious characters and events. Lynch has said, "It's better not to know so much about what things mean or how they might be interpreted or you'll be too afraid to let things keep happening."

Lynch does not consider himself a perfectionist, but he insists on having things his way. "You can't make compromises," he said. "Compromises kill the film." But while Lynch is demanding about how his movies are made, cast members love working with him. Actor Don Davis said about Lynch, "In the time I knew him, no matter what happened on the set, no matter what went wrong, I never ever heard him raise his voice or be cruel to anyone." To him, Lynch is completely normal; he just likes making movies that aren't.

FUNNY MAN

If comic actor Dana Carvey doesn't seem like himself, don't worry. That's his job. He's known for playing memorable characters and performing uncanny celebrity impersonations.

Carvey was born in Missoula in 1955, the fourth of five children. His parents were both teachers. He was a shy child who spent lots of time alone doing impersonations and creating imaginary characters. He also acted in some high school plays.

After high school, Carvey attended San Francisco State University. He majored in radio and television broadcasting, and continued practicing his impersonations and comedy routines. While he was still in college, Carvey got up the courage to try his act in front of an audience. He was soon performing at comedy clubs in the area and eventually won the San Francisco Stand-Up Comedy

Dana Carvey is uncomfortable with fame. "I've always been able to kind of skirt it . . . because I played characters," he says. "I was sort of invisible in my costume."

Competition. By the time he graduated, he knew what he wanted to do. He moved to Los Angeles to look for work as a comic actor.

Carvey has appeared in many movies, but he is best known for his work on the television show *Saturday Night Live*. He was a member of the cast from 1986 to 1992. During that time, he created such popular characters as the Church Lady and the grumpy old man on "Weekend Update." Carvey's hilarious characters have earned him six Emmy nominations. He took home the prize in 1993.

DINOSAUR HUNTER

Millions of years ago, all of eastern Montana was a giant swamp, home to great herds of dinosaurs. Jack Horner, who was born in Shelby, Montana, is one of the country's leading authorities on dinosaurs. Working from his base at the Museum of the Rockies in Bozeman, he often leads digs around the state.

Horner has been digging up fossils—rocks with the remains of ancient animals in them—since he was eight years old. Dinosaurs fascinated him then, and they still do. Horner was not especially successful in school, but he always did well in science classes. He

In 2000, Jack Horner and other scientists from the Museum of the Rockies found five Tyrannosaurus rex skeletons in Montana. One of them was more than forty feet long.

says his brain is the "hunt, poke, and dig-around version issued to field scientists."

Some of the fossils Horner has found have changed what scientists believe about the way dinosaurs lived. For example, they may have been quite sociable. He has also suggested that massive Tyrannosaurus rex may have been more of a scavenger than a hunter.

After discovering a nearly intact dinosaur egg, Horner became interested in the life of mother dinosaurs and their young. He has found an entire nest of Maiasaura fossils on Egg Mountain in north-central Montana. There's always more to learn, so Horner keeps digging.

LEADING THE WAY

The first Crow woman to earn a doctorate degree, Janine Pease–Pretty On Top has made sure she won't also be the last. She worked on the Crow Indian Reservation for twenty years to build Little Big Horn College from a tiny school to a thriving junior college with many successful graduates.

When she started working at Little Big Horn College, the school had thirty-two students and three staff members. During her years as the school's president, it grew to include more than three hundred students and a staff of forty. Pease–Pretty On Top says the key is making education meaningful to the students. "We try to match the school to the community—kind of like a spider on a mirror," she says. "Arts, music, and the lore of the Crow Nation are at the heart of our program and about 25 percent of our classes are in the Crow

Janine Pease-Pretty On Top, the first Crow woman to earn a doctoral degree, believes, "Native people must pursue, acquire and own knowledge to achieve freedom: otherwise we are mere slaves."

language."

Pease–Pretty on Top has won a "genius grant" from the MacArthur Foundation, the Jeannette Rankin Civil Liberties Award, and the National Indian Education Association's Educator of the Year Award. But her greatest reward, she says, is seeing students succeed in education and life. "It's a huge success when we have a graduate," she says. "Every time we have a graduate, we get somebody off welfare."

As a boy, another Crow Indian named Plenty Coups walked to the Crazy Mountains hoping to see a vision. After days of praying and fasting, he had a dream in which herds of buffalo disappeared before him, replaced by strange animals. He also saw a dark forest with storm clouds gathering overhead. He later recalled, "[I] saw the beautiful trees twist like blades of grass and fall in tangled piles. . . . Only one tree, tall and straight, was left standing."

On returning to his village, he asked the tribal elders what the

Plenty Coups convinced many of his fellow Crows to work with white men rather than fighting them.

dream meant. They told him that the strange animals were the white man's cattle, the forest was the Native American people, and the storm was the white man. The one tree left standing, they said, was the Crow people—the only tribe never to declare war on the white man. They also told him that he would live a long life and become a great chief.

Plenty Coup's dream convinced many Crow Indians to accept the presence of white men. As a young man, he fought the enemies of the Crow, often alongside whites. He distinguished himself on the battlefield, and eventually became chief of his tribe.

As chief, Plenty Coups often represented his people as a diplomat rather than as a soldier. He encouraged the Crow people to learn farming, and he traveled to Washington, D.C., many times to lobby for educational and economic support for the Crow. Thanks to his leadership, the Crow fared better than many other Native American groups. Plenty Coups also gave more of himself to the U.S. government. When World War I broke out, he encouraged his people to join the army. "When the war is over," he said, "the soldier-chiefs will not forget that the Crows came to their aid."

After the war ended, Plenty Coups again traveled to Washington. This time, he joined President Warren G. Harding at Arlington National Cemetery for the burial of the Unknown Soldier. The chief was dressed in beaded buckskin and an eagle-feather headdress. He removed his war bonnet and laid it on the tomb, then said: "I am glad to represent all the Indians of the United States in placing on the grave of this noble warrior this . . . war bonnet, every eagle feather of which represents a deed of valor by my race. I hope the Great Spirit will grant that these noble warriors have not given up their lives in vain and that there will be peace to all men hereafter."

Plenty Coups lived from 1848 to 1932. In that time, he saw his people's way of life change completely. Just as his elders had predicted, he had become a great chief and lived a long life. His leadership helped the Crow people prepare for the future. Says Janine Pease–Pretty On Top, "We still live and benefit from the vision that he had."

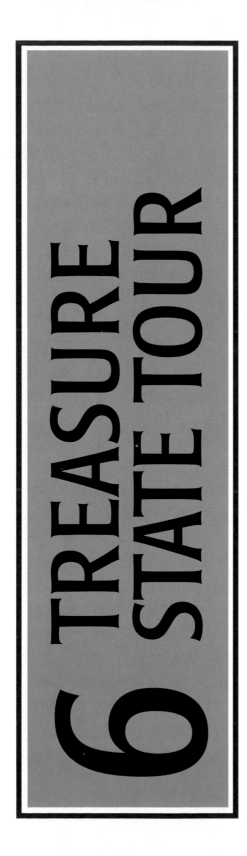

6 TREASURE STATE TOUR

Many people say Montana is so big and its eastern and western parts are so different that it should be two states instead of one. Trout-fishing streams in the mountain valleys are nothing like the empty prairies of east-central Montana. Rugged peaks that rise above every town in the northwest seem a world away from the badlands of the southeast.

Yet every feature of the Montana landscape is a treasure of some kind. They add up to a bold and dramatic place. No wonder Montana is sometimes called the Treasure State.

THE NORTHWEST

Any tour of Montana should start with its best-known site, Glacier National Park. The park is famed for its majestic mountains, glowing lakes, and unspoiled beauty. The surroundings are so impressive that you can point a camera in any direction and get a good picture. More people visit Glacier than any other place in Montana.

There are only a few roads in the park, but dozens of hiking trails. These trails offer some of the best chances to see large wildlife anywhere in the country. One visitor was getting a good look at a mountain goat when suddenly it took off. "She came out of the trees right at me," he exclaimed. "I had to jump back to avoid

Mountain goats are a common sight in Glacier National Park.

being skewered." A surprising number of visitors even see grizzly bears tearing up old logs looking for food. Bears can be dangerous, though, so park rangers advise hikers to whistle or sing on the trails so bears know someone is coming and have time to hide or run away. Never surprise a bear!

In contrast to the dramatic sights of Glacier National Park, Flathead Lake to the south has a still, quiet air. Says one visitor, "Even the Oregonians in our group—who are used to beautiful landscapes—fell into a state of hushed awe."

Twenty-eight miles long and fifteen miles wide, Flathead Lake is the largest natural freshwater lake in the West. The lake is famous for

GOING-TO-THE-SUN ROAD

When Glacier became a national park in 1910, it was very difficult for anyone to travel through the park to enjoy it. To attract visitors, the state decided to build a road.

Glacier's mountain passes are so steep that some people thought building a road would be impossible. Hundreds of men moved thousands of tons of rock to create the road. The scenery around them was gorgeous but terrifying. One man who worked on the road later recalled, "On several occasions men stood at the top of the cliff, looked down the ladder, and turned in their resignations." It took eleven years, but in 1933 the brave men who didn't quit finally completed the Going-to-the-Sun Road.

Even today, the Going-to-the-Sun Road is an adventure to drive. In some places, it's nothing more than a ledge carved out of the mountainside. Vehicles longer than twenty-one feet or wider than eight feet (including mirrors) are not allowed on the steepest and narrowest sections of the road. The views are so amazing that many visitors prefer to ride on buses. This way, they can watch the breathtaking scenery and let someone else worry about driving off a cliff.

On a trip through the National Bison Range, you'll see bison and some fabulous scenery.

salmon and trout fishing and is popular with boaters, swimmers, and water-skiers. One highlight of Flathead Lake is Wild Horse Island, where there are indeed wild horses. There are also a lot of bighorn sheep and big birds, including ospreys, bald eagles, and red-tailed hawks.

In the early 1800s, millions of bison lived on the Great Plains. By 1900, fewer than a thousand remained. Most of the surviving bison were in or near Montana. In 1908, 19,000 acres in the Flathead

PLACES TO SEE

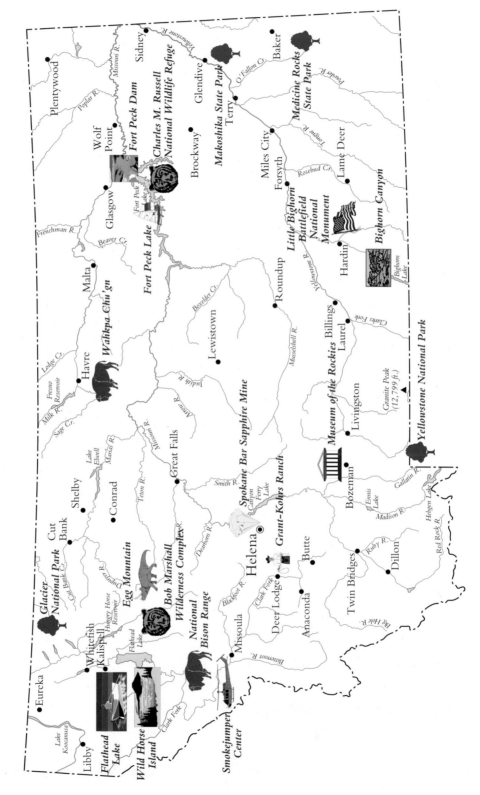

Eureka

Libby

Flathead Lake

Lake
Koocanusa

Wild Horse Island

Whitefish
Kalispell

Flathead
Lake

Glacier National Park

Cut
Bank

Cut Bank Cr.

Hungry Horse
Reservoir

Dupuyer R.

Egg Mountain

*Bob Marshall
Wilderness Complex*

Teton R.

*National
Bison Range*

Missoula

Deer Lodge

Anaconda

Butte

Bitterroot R.

Blackfoot R.

Clark Fork

Clark Fork

*Smokejumper
Center*

Shelby

Conrad

Lake
Elwell

Marias R.

Great Falls

Missouri R.

Smith R.

Spokane Bar Sapphire Mine

Canyon
Ferry
Lake

Helena

Grant-Kohrs Ranch

Twin Bridges

Ruby R.

Dillon

Red Rock R.

Ennis
Lake

Madison R.

Hebgen Lake

Big Hole R.

Havre

Wahkpa Chu'gn

Malta

Milk R.

Fresno
Reservoir

Lodge Cr.

Sage Cr.

Frenchman R.

Beaver Cr.

Glasgow

Wolf
Point

Fort Peck Dam

Fort Peck
Lake

Fort Peck Lake

*Charles M. Russell
National Wildlife Refuge*

Brockway

Judith R.

Arrow Cr.

Lewistown

Boxelder Cr.

Roundup

Musselshell R.

Plentywood

Poplar R.

Missouri R.

Sidney

Yellowstone R.

Glendive

Makoshika State Park

Terry

O'Fallon Cr.

Baker

*Medicine Rocks
State Park*

Powder R.

Miles City

Forsyth

Rosebud Cr.

Tongue R.

Lame Deer

*Little Bighorn
Battlefield
National
Monument*

Hardin

Yellowstone R.

Bighorn Canyon

Bighorn
Lake

Billings

Laurel

Clarks Fork

Museum of the Rockies

Bozeman

Livingston

Granite Peak
(12,799 ft.)

Gallatin R.

Yellowstone National Park

Valley were set aside for the bison to run free. Today, the National Bison Range is home to about 450 of the shaggy beasts. You can walk along a nature trail, but no people are allowed on the open range. The bison prefer it that way.

Northwestern Montana is also the site of the Bob Marshall Wilderness Complex. The Bob, as it is known, covers more than 1.5 million acres of wilderness. It is home to elk, deer, grizzly bears, and wolves. Patient visitors may also see bighorn sheep, cougars, lynxes, bobcats, and otters. As a wilderness area rather than a park, the Bob has no recreation facilities. Instead, it offers some of the most beautiful and challenging hiking trails in the state. If you can get by without shelter, electricity, or plumbing, the Bob is an ideal place for camping, climbing, rafting, and snowshoeing.

In 1841, Father Pierre-Jean De Smet built a mission church in the Bitterroot Valley, surrounded by gentle mountain peaks. This mission, in what is now Stevensville, was the first attempt at a European settlement in Montana. The church was abandoned in 1850, but it was rebuilt in 1866 by Father Anthony Ravalli. Today, the simple church looks very much like it did then. And visitors can still see the same sweeping view of the Bitterroot Mountains that inspired Father De Smet to settle there nearly 170 years ago.

After all this wild outdoors, you might want to stop in Missoula to get a taste of city life. Missoula is a pleasant, lively city, filled with restaurants and handsome buildings from a hundred years ago. It seems to combine the best of everything—a sophisticated city in the middle of the wilderness.

While you're in town, be sure to visit at the Smokejumper Center, the nation's largest training center for smokejumpers, the people who parachute in to fight forest fires. The center is filled with videos and exhibits about the dangerous job. You can also climb to the top of a reconstructed fire lookout tower. Perhaps you'll even see a plane full of smokejumpers heading out to a fire.

THE SOUTHWEST

In 1859, a man named Johnny Grant built a house in a grassy part of southwestern Montana and started grazing cattle there. Over the years, the ranch thrived. Today, what is known as the Grant-Kohrs Ranch is a national historic site. Visitors can tour the elegant ranch house and explore the blacksmith shop, bunkhouse, and other ranch buildings, where park rangers talk about the hard work of the West's early ranchers. The best time to visit the ranch is during the Western Heritage Days in July. Members of the ranch staff show how to groom horses, round up cattle, brand calves, and harvest hay. There are also blacksmithing demonstrations, wagon rides, and old-time cooking from a real chuck wagon.

If you want to find real treasure during your trip around the Treasure State, head to the Spokane Bar Sapphire Mine next to Hauser Lake. Amid the bare hills and scrubby juniper bushes, visitors dig through gravel looking for sapphires. Not everyone finds them, and the ones they find may not be very big, but people keep trying. One visitor noted, "My husband, my girls, and I were there this past Monday and Tuesday. We found 20 sapphires totaling 38 carats, many of them 2 carats and over. We had a great time!" The largest sapphire found there weighed 155 carats. People have also found garnets, diamonds, topaz, and rubies.

Visitors enjoy a wagon ride around the Grant-Kohrs Ranch.

After searching for your own treasure you may want to check out Bannack, the site of Montana's first major gold rush. Walking down the ghost town's dusty streets is an eerie experience. Any moment, you expect a tumbleweed to roll by or a stagecoach to come roaring around a corner. After gold was discovered there in 1862, the population jumped from zero to more than three thousand in just one year. More than fifty buildings from the gold rush days are still standing, including houses, a church, and Montana's first jail. Some people say the hotel is the most photographed spot in Montana. If you want to see Bannack at its liveliest, visit during Bannack Days in July. The festival includes stagecoach rides, a fake gunfight on main street, and old-time dancing.

Many miners who left Bannack headed for Helena, where gold had been discovered at Last Chance Gulch in 1864. So many people struck it rich there that by 1888, Helena was home to fifty millionaires. It was the wealthiest city per person in the nation. Much of Helena's past is still visible, from the millionaires' lavish mansions to one-room buildings that once housed miners. Another Helena highlight is the Cathedral of St. Helena. This glittering church boasts two towers, each 230 feet tall, a white marble altar, and amazing stained glass windows from Germany.

Before leaving Montana's old mining region, stop by Butte to see Berkeley Pit. Once the nation's largest open-pit copper mine, it is now a huge mess. It's 1,800 feet deep and a mile across and filling with water—poisonous water. Birds have died from landing in the water, which is a strange greenish color from the copper. The pit is a vivid reminder of what people can do to the land.

NORTH-CENTRAL MONTANA

Just east of the jagged Rocky Mountain Front is a dry and windy land of grass-covered hills and plains. Today, the area produces a tremendous amount of wheat and barley. But long before humans settled here, it was dinosaur country. Scientists have found entire nests of dinosaur eggs at Egg Mountain, which gave them a lot of clues about the behavior of the ancient creatures. Egg Mountain is

The people of Helena are proud of their elegant cathedral.

the site of the world's first discovery of dinosaur eggs with tiny dinosaurs in them. Visitors can tour the dig sites. Some even sign up to help unearth the fossils.

Before Native Americans had horses or guns, they used a simple method to kill bison. They would wait until a herd of bison was near a cliff, then startle the animals near the back of the herd. The bison would stampede, and some would be unable to stop running before they reached the cliff. They would fall to their death below.

Cliffs like these are called buffalo jumps or bison kill sites. The largest and best-preserved bison kill site on the Montana plains is Wahkpa Chu'gn. At the site, you can see displays of artifacts found there and learn more about how Indians used buffalo. "It really makes you think about how smart and tough people had to be back then," said one visitor. "How many people today would know how to kill a buffalo with no weapons, butcher it so nothing is wasted, and use its hide to keep warm in a Montana winter?"

Wahkpa Chu'gn is in a place where you wouldn't usually expect to find ancient history sites. Instead of being miles from the nearest highway, it's located behind a mall in the town of Havre.

SOUTH-CENTRAL MONTANA

South-central Montana offers some of the state's wildest scenery— and some of its best fishing. People come from all over the world to fish in the Yellowstone and Madison Rivers. But even if you're not a fisher, you'll find plenty to do in this part of Montana.

If you like dinosaurs, the Museum of the Rockies in Bozeman is a good place to start. You can watch experts prepare fossils or check

THE MOUNTAIN MAN RENDEZVOUS

History comes to life each summer just north of Red Lodge. At the Mountain Man Rendezvous history lovers get together to recreate the world of the trappers and traders. The event brings back the sights, sounds, smells, and flavors of long ago.

In the 1800s, mountain men gathered once a year to sell goods and stock up on supplies for the coming year. The Mountain Man Rendezvous continues that tradition. During the gathering, participants buy and sell goods at Trader's Row. Sellers must dress in the clothing of the time. And they can only sell goods that were available then, such as beadwork, dolls, and handmade knives. The event also includes musical performances, reenactments, and demonstrations of old-fashioned skills such as blacksmithing and shooting black-powder rifles.

In the nineteenth century, a rendezvous usually included gambling, robberies, fistfights, and shootings. Gunfights break out at today's rendezvous too, but they are always staged. As the event's organizers say, "Everybody is shooting blanks, and we all have dinner together later on."

out an exhibit with an animated triceratops looking for food. At the museum you can also learn about how the Rockies were formed and about the people who have lived there through the centuries.

To see the best of the Rockies, head to Red Lodge. There you can get on the Beartooth Highway, which journalist Charles Kuralt called, "the most beautiful roadway in America." The road has so many steep climbs and hairpin turns that drivers need three hours to travel less than seventy miles. At its highest point, the road reaches an elevation of nearly 11,000 feet. The road is so high that it can snow there anytime—even in July. You never know when you might get into a snowball fight. From the summit, you can see for miles. All around you are glaciers, meadows, and mountaintops—including Granite Peak, the tallest mountain in Montana.

Driving the Beartooth Highway would be worth it even without the incredible views because it leads to Yellowstone National Park. The world's first national park, Yellowstone contains jagged canyons and dramatic waterfalls. But it is probably most famous for colorful boiling hot springs and shooting geysers. Most of the park is in Wyoming, but a section of it is in Montana, and three of its five entrances are there.

THE EAST

Eastern Montana is a world apart. The land is dry, flat, and bare. In some places, you can travel for miles without seeing a tree or a hill, much less a forest or mountain. Instead, there are just the plains with a sky that never seems to end. This kind of scenery takes some getting used to, but once that happens many people find they can't get it out of their minds.

A dam may not seem like an interesting place to visit, but Fort Peck Dam in the northeast is worth a trip. It stands as a monument to human achievement. The dam is 21,026 feet long and 250

Cliffs tower a thousand feet above the river in Bighorn Canyon.

When future president Theodore Roosevelt saw Medicine Rocks in 1883, he called it "as fantastically beautiful a place as I have ever seen; it seemed impossible that the hand of man should not have something to do with the formation."

feet high at its tallest point. While it was being built in the 1930s, the dam provided work for 50,000 people.

Fort Peck Dam backed up the waters of the Missouri River to create Fort Peck Lake, which stretches for 134 miles. The huge expanse of water makes fishers happy, as the lake is full of walleye, sauger, smallmouth bass, lake trout, chinook salmon, and northern pike.

Fort Peck Lake is entirely surrounded by the Charles M. Russell National Wildlife Refuge, which protects the most intact section of all the northern plains. This rugged country is no gentle grassland. Instead, it is a maze of bluffs, buttes, and ravines. This is hard land for people to live in, but elk, bighorn sheep, pronghorn, and countless other animals thrive here.

Eastern Montana also has some rough land. At Makoshika State Park just outside of Glendive, strange pillars and buttes have been formed by wind and water eating away the land. Farther south, at Medicine Rocks State Park, the wind has carved holes and tunnels in huge rocks standing alone on the grasslands. The effect is eerie but beautiful.

Another beautiful spot is Bighorn Canyon National Recreation Area, where cliffs tower above Bighorn Lake. Boaters can't get enough of Bighorn Canyon, but the area also attracts wildlife lovers, who come to see bald eagles and peregrine falcons swooping through the sky.

Let's end our tour of the Treasure State at the site of the most famous event in Montana's history, the Battle of the Little Bighorn. When you visit Little Bighorn Battlefield National Monument today, you might wonder why such a dry, treeless place was so important to the Indians or the U.S. government. In fact, the site itself was not very important. It was simply one of the places where the two cultures fought for control of the land—and the future.

Looking around from the headstones on Last Stand Hill or the 7th Cavalry Monument, you see nothing but the Little Bighorn River and some grass-covered hills. Most of the year, the grass is dry and brown. Only a square around the 7th Cavalry Monument and the visitor center are kept green. "This place keeps two things alive," one visitor commented. "The lawn and our memories."

THE FLAG: *The Montana flag displays the name of the state in large gold letters against a blue background. Below the name is the state seal. The flag was adopted in 1905.*

THE SEAL: *The seal, adopted in 1893, shows mountains and the Great Falls of the Missouri River as symbols of Montana's scenery. Below them are a plow, shovel, and pick, which represent farming and mining. The state motto appears at the base of the seal.*

STATE SURVEY

Statehood: November 8, 1889

Origin of Name: Montana comes from a Latin word meaning "mountainous"

Nicknames: Big Sky Country, Treasure State

Capital: Helena

Motto: *Oro y Plata* (Gold and Silver)

Animal: Grizzly bear

Bird: Western meadowlark

Fish: Blackspotted cutthroat trout

Flower: Bitterroot

Tree: Ponderosa pine

Stones: Sapphire, Montana agate

Fossil: Maiasaura (duck-billed dinosaur)

Grizzly bear

Bitterroot

MONTANA

Joseph Howard, the composer of several hundred popular songs, set Charles Cohan's words to music in 1910. The song was adopted as the official state song in 1945.

Words by Charles C. Cohan

Music by Joseph E. Howard

GEOGRAPHY

Highest Point: 12,799 feet above sea level, at Granite Peak

Lowest Point: 1,800 feet above sea level, along the Kootenai River in Lincoln County

Area: 147,047 square miles

Greatest Distance, North to South: 321 miles

Greatest Distance, East to West: 559 miles

Bordering States: Idaho to the west, Wyoming to the south, North Dakota and South Dakota to the east.

Hottest Recorded Temperature: 117° F at Glendive on July 20, 1893 and at Medicine Lake on July 5, 1937

Coldest Recorded Temperature: −70° F at Rogers Pass on January 20, 1954

Average Annual Precipitation: 15 inches

Major Rivers: Bighorn, Bitterroot, Blackfoot, Clark Fork, Flathead, Gallatin, Jefferson, Kootenai, Madison, Milk, Missouri, Musselshell, Powder, Sun, Yellowstone

Major Lakes: Bighorn, Canyon Ferry, Flathead, Fort Peck, Hebgen, Hungry Horse, Medicine, Tiber

Trees: alder, ash, aspen, birch, cedar, fir, larch, pine, spruce

Wild Plants: aster, blue grama, buffalo grass, columbine, daisy, dryad, lily, lupine, poppy, primrose, western wheatgrass

Animals: bear, beaver, bighorn sheep, bison, deer, elk, mink, moose, mountain goat, muskrat, pronghorn antelope

Birds: bluebird, duck, eagle, goose, grouse, magpie, partridge, pheasant, swan, wren

Fish: crappie, grayling, perch, sturgeon, trout, whitefish

Endangered Animals: black-footed ferret, Eskimo curlew, gray wolf, least tern, pallid sturgeon, white sturgeon, whooping crane

Gray wolf

TIMELINE

Montana History

1700s Assiniboine, Blackfeet, Crow, Gros Ventre, Flathead, Kalispel, Kootenai, and Northern Cheyenne Indians live in Montana

1743 The first European explorers known to enter Montana, François and Louis-Joseph de la Vérendrye, cross the state's southeastern corner

1803 Eastern Montana becomes U.S. territory when the United States buys the Louisiana Purchase

1805–1806 American explorers Meriwether Lewis and William Clark pass through Montana on their way to the Pacific Ocean and back

1807 Montana's first fur trading post is built at the mouth of the Bighorn River

1841 Father Pierre-Jean De Smet, a Catholic priest, founds St. Mary's Mission, the first European settlement in Montana

1857 Sheep ranching begins in the Bitterroot Valley

1862 Gold is discovered at Grasshopper Creek, near Bannack

1864 Montana Territory is created

1876 Sioux, Cheyenne, and Arapaho Indians defeat U.S. troops led by George Armstrong Custer at the Battle of the Little Bighorn

1879 The Utah & Northern Railway becomes the first railroad to reach Montana

1881 Copper king Marcus Daly begins mining operations near Butte

1889 Montana becomes the 41st state

1910 Glacier National Park is established

1916 Jeannette Rankin of Missoula is elected to the U.S. House of Representatives, becoming the first woman to serve in Congress

1917 A fire on Granite Mountain near Butte kills 168 copper miners

1940 Montana workers complete Fort Peck Dam

1951 Oil wells begin operating in eastern Montana

1955 Montana's first aluminum plant begins processing in Columbia Falls

1967–1968 Butte metal miners hold an eight-month strike, the longest in Montana history

1969 Open-pit mining for coal begins in southeastern Montana

1972 Montana voters approve a new state constitution

1988 Forest fires destroy large stands of Montana timber during a draught

1994 The U.S. government agrees to protect 1.7 million acres of western Montana land from commercial use

ECONOMY

Agricultural Products: barley, beef cattle, dairy products, hay, mustard, oats, potatoes, safflower, sheep, sugar beets, sunflowers, wheat

Barley

Manufactured Products: fertilizer, food products, machinery, refined oil, wood products

Natural Resources: barite, clay, coal, copper, gold, gypsum, lead, limestone, lumber, molybdenum, natural gas, oil, platinum, silver, uranium, zinc

Business and Trade: healthcare, real estate, transportation, wholesale and retail trade

CALENDAR OF CELEBRATIONS

Race to the Sky Montana's toughest dogsled drivers brave the cold each February, racing from Lincoln to Holland Lake and back.

National Ski-Joring Finals This March competition in Red Lodge promotes a sport imported from Norway, where horse-drawn skiers swoosh over the snow past obstacles and over jumps.

St. Patrick's Day Butte celebrates its Irish roots on March 17 as pipers, drummers, and dancers dressed in green parade through the streets.

Bucking Horse Sale Miles City kicks off the rodeo season in May with a professional bucking bronco sale. Watch expert cowboys try to bust each horse—the ones that buck the best are bought for rodeos.

International Wildlife Film Festival Mountain lions and grizzly bears play starring roles at this unusual film festival each spring, when Missoula theaters show the world's best wild animal movies.

Sleeping Giant Swing and Jazz Jubilee The streets of Helena rock with the sounds of Dixieland jazz for a week each June.

Yellowstone Boatfloat For three days in July, boaters follow the route Lewis and Clark took down the Yellowstone River for 110 miles between Livingston and Columbus. Anyone can join the fun using any kind of boat, from a rubber raft to a homemade canoe.

Milk River Indian Days The Gros Ventre and Assiniboine tribes hold a pow-wow the last weekend in July at Fort Belknap. Dancing, athletic contests, and traditional foods are popular at the festival.

Sweet Pea Festival Each August, Bozeman celebrates the arts with outdoor concerts, craft displays, and a big parade.

Crow Fair and Rodeo Indians from all over North America camp along the Little Bighorn River in August, celebrating their heritage with parades, dancing, wild horse races, and an all-Indian rodeo.

Western Montana Fair Missoula holds one of the state's biggest country fairs in August. The fun includes old-fashioned events like a blacksmith competition and a longhorn cattle show.

Montana State Fair

Nordicfest Many of the families who live in Libby are descended from Norwegian settlers. In September the town gets back to its roots with a weekend of Scandinavian food, music, and dancing.

Montana Chokecherry Festival Lewistown celebrates a tiny, tangy, dark-red fruit that ripens in Montana each September. A pancake breakfast with chokecherry syrup and a pit-spitting contest are highlights of the event.

STATE STARS

Eric Bergoust (1969–   ) of Missoula is a champion aerial skier. A born daredevil, Bergoust started skiing over his own homemade jumps at age 13 and had joined the U.S. Ski Team by age 20. In 1998, his quadruple-twisting triple backflips brought him an Olympic gold medal. He also has three U.S. championships and seven World Cup victories under his belt.

Calamity Jane (1852?–1903) was one of the most colorful characters of the Wild West. Calamity Jane moved to Virginia City with her family during the gold rush of 1865. She worked as an army scout, prospector, and entertainer, and gained national fame while touring with Buffalo Bill's Wild West Show.

Calamity Jane

William A. Clark (1839–1925) was an industrialist whose business empire once spanned Montana. Clark's banking, transportation, manufacturing, and mining ventures helped shape the state's economy in the 19th century. A leader in Democratic politics, he served in the U.S. Senate from 1901 to 1905.

Gary Cooper (1901–1961) was a film star known for his good looks and strong, quiet style. Cooper grew up on a ranch near Helena and learned to ride horses at an early age. His handsome cowboy image landed him bit parts in Westerns during the 1920s, and by the 1930s he had become Hollywood's top box office draw. Cooper appeared in more than 80 movies during his lifetime, winning Academy Awards for his performance in *Sergeant York* and *High Noon*.

Gary Cooper

Marcus Daly (1841–1900), a Montana mining tycoon, moved to the United States from Ireland when he was 15. He went west, became an expert miner, and bought a claim to the Anaconda silver mine near Butte. The mine contained a huge vein of copper that made Daly rich in just a few years. Daly also built many Montana banks, power plants, and railroads. In the 1890s, he fought William A. Clark for control of state politics in what was known as the war of the copper kings.

Ivan Doig (1939–   ) writes vivid stories about Montana and its people. Doig was born in White Sulphur Springs, where his parents were ranch hands. Life in the rural West became the subject of many of his novels. His best-known books include *English Creek* and *This House of Sky*.

A. B. Guthrie, Jr. (1901–1991), who grew up in Choteau, wrote novels about the western frontier. Guthrie was one of the first writers to make life in the Old West seem as harsh as it really was. In 1947, he published

The Big Sky, a realistic novel about the days of the mountain men. He won a Pulitzer Prize for his 1949 novel *The Way West*.

A. B. Guthrie, Jr.

Jack Horner (1946–   ) is one of the world's leading dinosaur hunters. Born in Shelby, Horner started digging up fossils when he was in grade school. As an adult, Horner has discovered many amazing fossils, including a nest of baby dinos and several Tyrannosaurus rex skeletons. Working at Montana's Museum of the Rockies, he does research on the everyday life of Tyrannosaurus rex and others its size.

Chet Huntley (1911–1974) was a leading television newscaster. A native of Cardwell, Huntley began his career as a radio announcer in Seattle. He moved to television in 1951. In 1956, Huntley teamed up with David Brinkley on a nightly 15-minute news program called the *Huntley-Brinkley Report*. The highly rated show won eight Emmy Awards over the next 14 years. Huntley was named Broadcaster of the Year in 1970, just before retiring to Montana.

Dorothy M. Johnson (1905–1984) wrote many gritty, realistic stories about life in the Wild West. Johnson grew up in Whitefish, graduated from the

University of Montana, and worked as a magazine editor in New York for many years. Her first works of fiction appeared in the 1940s, in the *Saturday Evening Post* and other magazines. Her stories "The Hanging Tree," "A Man Called Horse," and "The Man Who Shot Liberty Valance" were made into popular films.

Evel Knievel (1938–), a native of Butte, is a motorcyclist whose death-defying stunts have made him a legend. Evel Knievel's career started in 1965, with attention-getting acts like riding through fire and jumping over mountain lions. Each year his feats got more incredible. In 1974, he tried to jump Idaho's Snake River Canyon on a rocket-powered "sky-cycle." He just missed the edge and parachuted to the canyon floor. By the time he retired in 1975, he had cleared 13 Mack trucks, sailed over 14 Greyhound buses, and broken 35 bones.

Evel Knievel

Myrna Loy (1905–1993) was a movie actress who charmed millions with her elegant wit and style. Born Myrna Williams in Radersburg, she spent her childhood in Helena, where she made her stage debut with a dance routine at age 12. After moving with her family to Los Angeles, she began acting in local theater, then in movies. In the 1930s, her role as Nora Charles in *The Thin Man* made her one of Hollywood's most popular stars.

Myrna Loy

Norman Maclean (1902–1990) wrote *A River Runs Through It and Other Stories*, a book about a Montana family that became the basis for a successful film. Maclean spent most of his youth in Missoula. He began writing late in life, but his depth and poetic style were immediately admired. A Montana firefighting tragedy is the subject of his last book, *Young Men and Fire*.

Dave McNally (1942–   ) was one of the top baseball pitchers of the 1960s and 1970s. Born in Billings, McNally started playing for the Baltimore Orioles in 1962, pitching a two-hit shutout in his first game. Between 1968 and 1972, he gained national fame with four 20-win seasons in a row. McNally was a powerful batter too. In 1970, he became the only pitcher ever to hit a grand slam in the World Series.

Plenty Coups (1848–1932) was a Crow Indian leader born near what is now Billings. When he was a young boy, he had a vision that told him white people would invade Crow lands. Believing the best way to help his people was to keep peace with the whites, he urged the Crow to join forces with the U.S. government in fighting their Indian enemies, the Sioux and Cheyenne. Plenty Coups was named chief of all the Crow in 1904.

Jeannette Rankin (1880–1973) was the first woman to serve in the U.S. Congress. Born near Missoula and educated at Montana State University, Rankin led the fight to get women the right to vote in Montana. In 1916, she was elected to the U.S. House of Representatives, where she supported the state's copper miners and campaigned for the right of all women in the United States to vote. Throughout her life, Rankin was also an active advocate for peace, opposing U.S. involvement in World War I, World War II, and Vietnam.

Jeannette Rankin

Martha Raye (1916–1994) was a popular singer and actress. Raye was born in Butte and began appearing on stage with her show business parents at age three. She later sang, acted in movies, and had her own television variety show. But Raye is best known for her generous spirit in entertaining troops during World War II. Beloved by thousands of U.S. war veterans, Raye won an Oscar for humanitarian service in 1969 and the Presidential Medal of Freedom in 1993.

Charles M. Russell (1864–1926) was an artist who captured the spirit of the West. Born in Missouri, Russell was sent to Montana at age 16 so he would learn about life the hard way. But Russell loved the West. He found work as a hunter, sheepherder, and cowboy. He began drawing and painting, recording what he saw and recreating famous western scenes. Russell eventually completed more than 4,000 works of cowboy art, and his romantic vision of the West is still strong today.

Harold Urey (1893–1981) was a pioneer in the field of atomic energy. Born in Walkerton, Indiana, Urey earned a bachelor's degree at the University of Montana. He was awarded the Nobel Prize in chemistry in 1934 for discovering deuterium, which was important in the development of nuclear power. During World War II, Urey helped create the world's first atomic bomb. Later he became active in the United Nations in the hope that the world would solve its problems more peacefully.

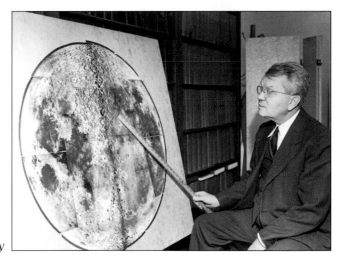

Harold Urey

Peter Voulkos (1924–   ) is an artist whose dramatic clay sculptures are in museums around the world. Born in Bozeman, Voulkos began working with clay as a student at Montana State College. He learned to make pots on a potter's wheel, then transformed them by tearing and gashing the surface of the clay. *The Rocking Pot* and *Gallas Rock* are among his best-known works.

James Welch

James Welch (1940–   ) is a poet and novelist who writes about modern Native American life. Welch's widely acclaimed books include *Winter in the Blood*, *Riding the Earthboy 40*, and *Fools Crow*, for which he won the American Book Award in 1986. He was born in Browning and is a member of the Blackfoot and Gros Ventre tribes.

Lones Wigger (1937–   ) is one of the world's most accurate marksmen. Wigger learned to shoot a rifle on his family's ranch near Great Falls. He joined the U.S. Army Marksmanship Unit and went on to win more than 100 international shooting awards, including two Olympic gold medals. Wigger is a member of the USA Shooting Hall of Fame.

Lones Wigger

TOUR THE STATE

Grizzly Discovery Center (West Yellowstone) You'll come face to face with Montana's most powerful beasts at this wildlife museum. Outdoor exhibits include live bears and wolves.

Little Bighorn Battlefield National Monument (Crow Agency) The Sioux, Cheyenne, and Arapaho Indians wiped out George Armstrong Custer and his troops here in 1876. More than 200 men who died in the battle are buried on Last Stand Hill.

Pictograph Cave State Park (Lockwood) Native American paintings created 5,000 years ago decorate the walls of an enormous cave here.

Moss Mansion (Billings) Banking king Preston Boyd Moss once owned this lavish home, which was completed in 1930. Much of Moss's elegant furniture is still on display.

Bighorn Canyon National Recreation Area (Fort Smith) Some of Montana's most breathtaking scenery can be found where 1,000-foot-high cliffs tower above Yellowtail Reservoir. Visit Devils Canyon Overlook for the most spectacular view.

Pryor Mountains Mysterious ice caves are hidden among the limestone peaks on the east side of Bighorn Canyon. Mustangs run free in the mountain's wild horse range.

Pompey's Pillar (Billings) Explorer William Clark carved his name at the foot of this stone landmark, naming it Pompy's Tower after the son of his Native American guide, Sacagawea.

Makoshika State Park (Glendive) The name of this wind-blown sandstone landscape comes from a Sioux word meaning "bad" or "stinking earth." The colorful rock formations are a great place to dig for dinosaur bones.

Range Riders Museum (Miles City) At this frontier museum you can visit a one-room schoolhouse, tour a tepee, and learn about Native American artwork, weapons, and tools.

Yellowstone National Park (Cooke City, Gardiner, and West Yellowstone) Only a small strip of this famous preserve lies in Montana, but you can enter the park from three locations in the Big Sky State. Its natural wonders include bears, beautiful lakes, and spouting geysers.

St. Mary's Mission (Stevensville) Montana's oldest Catholic mission was built in 1841. A church from 1866 marks the spot where the original building once stood.

C. M. Russell Museum (Great Falls) America's favorite cowboy artist had a studio in Great Falls. You can check out dozens of his oil paintings, watercolors, and sculptures at the exhibit hall next door.

Castle (White Sulphur Springs) This old silver mining camp once had 14 saloons. Today it's a ghost town, where you can wander among the crumbling buildings and imagine the secrets they hold.

Flathead Lake (Polson) Summer visitors enjoy boating, fishing and kayaking in these deep blue waters. Beautiful Wild Horse Island boasts bighorn sheep, wild horses, and 75 species of birds.

Smokejumpers Center (Missoula) This is the place where the bravest workers in the U.S. Forest Service learn to parachute into a blaze. Visitors can tour the parachuting base and learn how smokejumpers stop forest fires.

Glacier National Park (West Glacier) Called the Crown of the Continent, this

Grant-Kohrs Ranch

paradise high in the Rocky Mountains was once the homeland of the Salish, Kootenai, and Blackfoot Indians. Visitors love the Going-to-the-Sun Road, a narrow, winding route that takes them past towering peaks.

Ulm Pishkin State Monument (Great Falls) Hundreds of years ago, Indians drove herds of buffalo over the cliffs here. Today you can walk a trail along the cliffs and enjoy the view.

Grasshopper Glacier (Cooke City) Long ago, swarms of grasshoppers were trapped in the ice here. They can still be seen today.

Museum of the Rockies (Bozeman) The biggest attraction at this amazing museum are the fossils, including dinosaur eggs and a Tyrannosaurus rex skull.

Earthquake Lake (West Yellowstone) In 1959, a powerful earthquake caused a mountaintop to break off and fall into the Madison River, forming a lake full of huge boulders and drowned trees.

FUN FACTS

The world's shortest river, the Roe, connects Giant Springs with the Missouri River near Great Falls. The size of the Roe River shifts with the seasons, but at most it is 200 feet long.

Snowmelt from Triple Divide Peak in Glacier National Park flows toward three different corners of North America. Some of it ends up in the Pacific Ocean. The rest travels east to the Atlantic Ocean or north to Hudson Bay.

Montana towns like Offer, Opportunity, and Eureka have names that recall the state's mining boom days. But who knows how Big Arm, Square Butt, and Hungry Horse got their names.

FIND OUT MORE

If you'd like to find out more about Montana, check your local bookstore, library, or video store for these titles:

GENERAL STATE BOOKS

George, Charles, and Linda George. *Montana*. New York: Children's Press, 2000.

Thompson, Kathleen. *Montana*. Austin, TX: Raintree/Steck-Vaughn, 1996.

SPECIAL INTEREST BOOKS

Ancona, George. *Powwow*. New York: Harcourt Brace, 1993.

Blumberg, Rhoda. *The Incredible Journey of Lewis and Clark*. New York: Lothrop, Lee & Shepard, 1987.

Coyote Stories of the Montana Salish Indians. Helena: Montana Historical Society, 1999.

Patent, Dorothy Hinshaw. *Where the Bald Eagles Gather*. New York: Clarion, 1984.

Silverstein, Alvin, Virginia Silverstein, and Laura Silverstein Nunn. *The Grizzly Bear*. Brookfield, CT: Millbrook, 1998.

Stein, R. Conrad. *The Battle of the Little Bighorn*. New York: Children's Press, 1997.

Tarbescu, Edith. *The Crow*. New York: Franklin Watts, 2000.

VIDEOS

Montana on My Mind, 1994.

Wilderness USA: Montana, 1997.

INTERNET

www.discoveringmontana.com The official state website has lots of information on travel, history, and government and is loaded with links.

INDEX

Page numbers for illustrations are in boldface.